Praise for *Athletes Are Brands Too*

" We talk to our players all the time about the importance of using social media to build their brand. The position they're in as high-profile athletes comes with great responsibility that can influence others, lift people up and create a personal narrative. *Athletes Are Brands Too* provides a detailed guide for how athletes can begin to not only build their brand, but how to grow it, maximize it and [grasp] the importance of it. In a new world where social media has become the driving force of branding, I can't think of a more effective playbook for athletes to begin building their own message. "

—John Calipari, Naismith Memorial Basketball Hall of Famer

" A very insightful read for athletes at every level. "

—Ronnie Stanley, Professional Football Player

" Jeremy nails it again with this one. [My] copy [is] full of notes and high-lighted sections. I have a marketing background and learned so much in the first chapter alone that has impacted how I approach my job and interact with my readers and listeners. "

—Matt Miller, Bleacher Report

" An interesting read for athletes that can get them thinking about what inspires them, what motivates them, and what kind of legacy they want to leave when their time off the field is through. As an athlete you have an amazing opportunity to impact people—how you do it is up to you! This book gives you ideas on ways to achieve that. "

—Heather O'Reilly, Professional Soccer Player

" Great book . . . the numbers don't lie. "

—Jonathan Isaac, Professional Basketball Player

" Athletes, whether they realize it or not, are storytellers. With each tweet, video and comment their story is being shared with a massive community. Thus, Jeremy Darlow's book, *Athletes Are Brands Too*, is coming at the perfect time. This book offers a detailed gameplan to coach athletes on the role and responsibility they have as storytellers, while offering never-before-written guidance on the power their 'story' can have. This book is a gift to athletes and I would recommend anyone with a platform and desire to impact the world to read, underline, and carry his book everywhere. "
—Yogi Roth, Pac-12 Networks College Football Analyst, Award-Winning Storyteller, Expert Traveler

" If you are an athlete that wants to learn how to take your personal brand to the next level, then this is a must-read. Jeremy hits the nail on the head: a lot of us don't take advantage of the platform that we have to create success beyond our time in our respective sports. Personally I feel like I had plenty of knowledge in this area, but after reading this book I picked up even more of an understanding for the topic at hand. Athletes are brands too! We all have to hold each other accountable in grasping this concept so we can be free to continue living life long after our playing days are over. "
—Alvin Kamara, Professional Football Player

" This book is going to be a great educational tool for our student athletes. Jeremy has created a game plan that will teach athletes how to manage, market, and build their personal brands. I look forward to incorporating his ideas into our player development program. "
—Neal Brown, College Football Coach

" In uncertain times, Jeremy Darlow maps out how to control your look, your brand, and your future. This should be a textbook for the future of interaction in sports. "
—Dennis Dodd, CBS Sports Senior Columnist

" Great book. This is an athlete's guide to building a brand identity via social media and beyond. "

—Robert Griffin III, Professional Football Player

" I was not able to put this book down. I believe the way Jeremy conveyed the information about branding yourself is something that all professional athletes and athletes in general need to read. So important to learn how and why your brand is vital to your sustained success during and long after your playing career. Truly a must-read on branding! "

—Chamique Holdsclaw, Former Professional Basketball Player

" Relevant and timely. This book is filled with valuable lessons for today's athletes and athletic programs. "

—Manny Diaz, College Football Coach

" *Athletes Are Brands Too* delivers a candid and intriguing look at what it takes to build and to maintain a successful personal brand in sports. In an easy and fun read, Darlow breaks down how and why certain athletes become influencers. This book is not only insightful on the burgeoning power of social media, but it's also informative on the tools necessary to have a positive impact on an athlete's bottom line. It's an important read for any player looking for complete success. "

—Adrienne Lawrence, Sports Legal Analyst and Host

" Jeremy's inside information and writing style makes this book a must-read for every person and especially athletes that want to empower them-selves to fulfill all of their dreams beyond their respective field. "

—Ronny Turiaf, Former Professional Basketball Player

" I loved this book. Relevant, practical, easy to read and understand. "

—Kelly Graves, College Basketball Coach

" Jeremy's book is a must-read for any athlete—or influencer in general—trying to navigate the shark-infested waters of marketing, ambassadors, branding, and sponsorships. Whether you're in high school or on your rookie NBA deal, there's advice in there. He tells it like it is, and doesn't sugarcoat things, while drawing on his own personal experience from his time at adidas."

—**Martin Rickman,** UPROXX Sports + *Dime Magazine*

" This is the type of information an athlete like myself could spend an entire career learning...or, you could just read this book and gain the upper hand on how to market yourself.

In the life of an athlete, we sometimes are the hottest topic on the lips of fans, and the next day it feels like we are forgotten. It's important to take initiative to brand ourselves because people remember personality, not always performances. *Athletes Are Brands Too* lays it out simply: set yourself apart from the competition both on AND off the field, and you will shine. It tells you exactly how to do just that.

Fans remember personality just as much as performance, and nobody is going to do this for you. It's time to take initiative and create your personal brand."

—**Sandi Morris,** Olympic Silver Medalist, Pole Vault

" This book is dynamic. The use of real-world examples hit home with me."
—**Van Malone,** College Football Coach

**athletes
are brands
too**

athletes are brands too

How Brand Marketing Can Save Today's Athlete

Jeremy Darlow

jack + june
publishing

Jack and June Publishing, Portland, OR 97209

The publisher has made every effort to ensure that the information and statistics presented in this book were correct at press time.

Indigo: Editing, Design, and More
Cover design by Mako Miyamoto
Interior design by Paul Barrett, Girl Friday Productions

ISBN: 978-0-9996332-0-5

dedicated to
Greg & Shirley
Darlow
for always believing in me

1

your
influence

2

your
brand

3

your
voice

intro

If you're an athlete, I have some bad news for you: you don't matter—unless you can sell product or drive clicks. If you can't—if you don't have a strong personal brand—people simply won't care about you. The media won't care about you. Corporations (and their endorsement deals) won't care about you. If you don't have a last name like Bryant, Brady, or Jeter, you're just another John Doe.

Until now. Athletes have long been kept in the dark regarding one very important life lesson: how to build a personal brand.

Nearly 80 percent of NFL athletes are broke within their first two years out of the league. Why? In part because their personal brands are completely dependent on the sport they play and their athletic performance. That's all about to change. Brand marketing is a key to saving today's athlete. By building personal brands early on in their careers, athletes can create a value proposition that goes beyond sports performance, giving them a platform to succeed in life after the game.

This is the guidebook that will help you do just that.

In the next three chapters, you will learn how to build influence, beat the odds, and leverage your athletic accomplishments to construct a personal brand that transcends sports.

· · ·

Before we start, take a moment and write down the top-five greatest rebounders in NBA history.

Chances are you wrote down Dennis Rodman. Rodman is considered by many to be one of the greatest, if not *the* greatest, rebounders the game of basketball has ever seen. But statistically, Rodman is not even in the top twenty. His name sits behind unsung players like Buck Williams, Robert Parish, and Paul Silas. So why does Rodman come to mind before they do?

The answer is simple: Rodman has a stronger brand name.

Rodman's provocative brand was and is tied directly to rebounding, a specialized and often overlooked part of the game. A basketball niche, if you will. No one seemed to pay much attention to the rebound until the Worm— as he came to be known—started speaking out and dyeing his hair. Even those who didn't tune in to his games knew him by his off-the-court antics. The two-time all-star elevated a basketball commodity to headline news by building a polarizing personal brand that outshined his stats.

Since Rodman left the NBA, the rebound has once again returned to obscurity. That's no coincidence.

While I was a director of brand marketing for adidas, I was fortunate to work on marketing strategies and campaigns for some of the world's top athletes, such as Aaron Rodgers, Kris Bryant, Lionel Messi, and Von Miller. Part of my job was to understand the marketplace and the competition that operated within it. I had to think like my peers and anticipate their next moves as they related to athlete marketing and promotion. What I quickly realized is that the keepers of brands (people like me) are typically only concerned about the 1 percent. We are trained to seek out the cultural elite. But brand marketers are not alone in this thinking. We make up just a small portion of a population that also includes fans and media members who will ultimately determine your level of influence before, during, and after your athletic career. If you can't convince at least one of these segments that you are worth talking about, you're on a path to irrelevance. In the world of brand marketing, perception is everything.

What this could mean is, if you hit over thirty home runs and had thirty steals for a team not located in New York, Los Angeles, or Chicago, people may not care about you. If you racked up 1,200 receiving yards for a school outside of a "major" conference, people may not care about you. If you average twenty-one points per game but only have 25,000 Instagram followers, guess what? People may not care about you.

If you're not a member of the 1 percent, your chances of landing the cover of your favorite magazine are slim to none, and you can forget about a brand choosing you for a national television campaign. Our society cares about the most influential and recognizable athletes, who we believe can move the needle—guys like Kevin Durant, Cam Newton, and Mike Trout. And yes, I do realize I just named three men and no women. That's part of the problem.

But don't blame the media or the brand keepers themselves; they're doing exactly what they should be doing. If an athlete's brand isn't strong, if it won't sell more watches or bring in more readers, how does that partnership benefit the company or the journalist? The reality is that it doesn't.

It's on the athlete to make these organizations and the people who run them take notice.

So, as part of the 99 percent, what can you do to capture people's attention? The same thing Rodman did: Make us care. Make us talk. Make us remember.

Build a brand.

I can help. I know how brand marketers think. Not only am I one of them, but I'm also a genuinely concerned citizen who's tired of seeing people being boxed in or being undervalued for what they have accomplished. I'm tired of seeing athletes get excited about signing with a brand or a school only to be forgotten a few weeks later when their shot stops falling. And I'm so very tired of hearing about athletes going bankrupt or their lives falling apart after their sports careers end. It shouldn't be like that.

Athletes are so much more than points per game or yards after the catch or slugging percentage. These are people that our society sometimes worships and sometimes belittles. We forget that athletes are human. We forget that they bleed like we bleed and they cry like we cry. We forget that they have insecurities and baggage the same way that we do. We look at those who end up going broke and we shake our heads and call them failures. But the same way that college textbooks leave out life lessons to focus on skill or trade development, athletes are taught one thing: to be great at a particular sport and, in some cases, one single aspect of that sport. It's a recipe for success in athletics, not life.

The athlete's window of opportunity to make it playing a sport he or she has been perfecting since childhood grows smaller and smaller…until that window is gone. Forever. For a person whose entire life has been built around his or her ability to play a sport, what's left when that sport is done?

The brand.

That's why I wrote this book: to help athletes at every level build their personal brands and, as a result, prosperous lives rooted in what they're passionate about. Whether that passion is focused on a given sport or something outside of athletics altogether, it doesn't matter. Athletics can and should lead to a happy ending for each and every athlete.

This book is dedicated to teaching high school, college, and professional athletes how to leverage their influence and construct a personal brand that can overcome adversity, break through the clutter, and establish a unique position in the marketplace. All of these together can ultimately lead to success in *life*, not just sport. This isn't just another marketing book—it's one part road map, one part call to arms.

Rodman saw what others couldn't see, heard what others couldn't hear. The Worm cracked the code. Whether you average thirty points per game in the NBA or three, you're an influencer. How influential is up to you.

Athletes are brands too. Let's build yours.

1

your
influence

cattle call

Sitting in the lobby of the player hotel at the 2015 NFL Scouting Combine, I couldn't help but feel completely overwhelmed by brands—hundreds of them, on every floor of the facility. No, I'm not talking about adidas or Nike or Under Armour. I'm talking about brands like Jameis Winston, Marcus Mariota, Amari Cooper, and countless other aspiring athletes. All of these individuals were now focused on building their own personal brands in order to fulfill their dream of playing professional football. The attention had shifted from the name on the front of the jersey to the name on the back, and I couldn't help but wonder, *What took so long?* Why had the vast majority of these players waited until now to build and promote their personal brands?

The closer I looked, the more I realized it had nothing to do with the athletes themselves; rather, it had everything to do with the athletic environments they had been brought up in, environments that promote uniformity. The combine is the ultimate manifestation of that uniformity—a comprehensive athletic audition where every participating athlete undergoes a series of exhaustive mental and physical tests. The media has often described this as football's version of a cattle call, an event completely free of individuality. One by one, every participating athlete walked through the doors of the hotel. Each one wore the exact same event-issued sweat suit, differentiated only by the position and numbers that had been screen-printed onto their shirts.

The more players I saw make their way through the hotel, the more anxious I became. Here I was at an event sometimes referred to as "the most important job interview of your life," and it wasn't until this moment that many of these athletes were working on inserting themselves into the minds of the people who held their futures in their hands. The players had no idea what they were leaving on the table by not building their brands sooner. No one had prepared them, so how could we expect each athlete to suddenly turn it on? To instantly understand what it means to build a personal brand and portray that brand in a way that wins over every general manager and media outlet in attendance? That's not how marketing works. It's not a switch you can flip. Brands are not built in a day, nor are brand managers.

It was in that moment that I knew something could and should be done. Sports are doing what they need to do in order to grow. Leagues are doing the same. And I don't fault them for it. It's business. But athletes shouldn't be left behind. It's time athletes treated themselves as brands, just like the sports they play and the leagues they play for do.

follow the leader

This book is meant to be an agent for change and a catalyst for an athlete movement built around personal branding. But before we get into it, we need some inspiration. I'm about to preach to you the importance of building a personal brand, and for that, I need *the* shining example. The brand every athlete has uttered or thought about at one point in his or her life. The brand every parent or coach reading this book knows. The brand that can be seen or heard or felt from every angle. Whether it's in the news, through social media, or on television, the brand that is always there.

And I know just the one: Kardashian.

It's a name that has always fascinated me as a brand marketer. Like it or not, we're all very familiar with it. The person responsible (and our inspiration) is Kris Jenner. Yes, I'm serious. The matriarch of the Kardashian family is the brains behind the empire that, as BuzzFeed put it, "manipulated the media to become the most famous family in the world." Love them or hate them, the Kardashians have built a brand that has changed the way we think about marketing.

What Jenner and her family have created is nothing short of remarkable. The results speak for themselves. Her show, *Keeping Up with the Kardashians*, first aired on October 14, 2007, and has since become one of the longest-running reality television shows of all time. Jenner's goal was simple, as she put it in her autobiography:

> Every time we renewed for another season, I would think to myself, "How can I take these fifteen minutes of fame and turn them into thirty?"

She had a vision, and her family has reaped the rewards.

Look up your favorite athlete on Twitter or Instagram. How many followers do they have? Kim Kardashian West has more. At the time of this writing, Mrs. Kardashian West sat at over 55 million followers on Twitter and a remarkable 103 million followers on Instagram. Her sisters are no slouches either. Khloé Kardashian has over 24 million followers on Twitter and 69 million on Instagram, while Kourtney Kardashian has the "smallest"(!) following among the sisters with over 22 million on Twitter and 58 million on Instagram.

SOCIAL MEDIA AUDIENCES		Instagram	Twitter
	Kim Kardashian West	103MM followers	55.3MM followers
	Khloé Kardashian	69MM	24.8MM
	Kourtney Kardashian	58.5MM	22.9MM
	Stephen Curry	17.5MM	10.3MM
	Odell Beckham, Jr.	8.9MM	2.73MM
	Kobe Bryant	7.5MM	12.5MM
	Serena Williams	6.4MM	9.19MM
	Cam Newton	3.9MM	1MM
	New York Yankees	1.6MM	2.69MM

Note: Numbers are accurate as of September 6, 2017.

Look at those numbers and tell me Kris Jenner and her family aren't brilliant brand minds. Look at those numbers and tell me these women have no talent. The best brand marketers in the world are the people we find ourselves talking about without being quite sure why. People like the Kardashians.

The success or failure of your brand will depend on your ability to get people talking about you, thinking about you, wanting to be you while you're off the field as much as while you're on it.

athletes are brands too

Your aptitude for playing a sport at a high level has provided you with an opportunity that the average person is not afforded. But the iron isn't hot for long, so you had better strike fast. This window of influence represents your fifteen minutes of fame. Fifteen minutes that, through the lessons learned in this book, we're going to stretch to thirty.

Just like the Kardashians did.

the new world

Brand building today in no way resembles that of twenty years ago, and that's good news for everyone reading this book. Two decades ago a person could clearly identify the most popular and most influential athletes in sports. Typically those positions correlated directly with performance. The most talented athletes tended to also be the most talked about: Michael Jordan, Shaquille O'Neal, and Charles Barkley in the NBA and John Elway, Jerry Rice, and Deion Sanders in the NFL. These athletes dominated the conversation because the media set the public narrative and television dictated content consumption. Essentially the media played puppet master in prescribing what we talked about and whom we rooted for.

The advent of social media has changed all of that. Power has shifted from the networks and news outlets to the individual. To you. The possibilities presented to this generation of athletes are infinite. Celebrity attainment has been revolutionized, and according to the *Huffington Post*, it doesn't appear that we'll ever go back to the way things were: "With fewer young people watching TV, the internet is the new place for overnight stardom."

To demonstrate how things have changed, let's conduct a blind taste test of sorts. In the diagram below, draw a line connecting the professional football résumé with what you would expect to be the NFL athlete's corresponding Twitter following.

> **❝ The internet is the new place for overnight stardom. ❞** *Huffington Post*

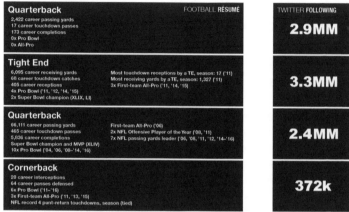

Quarterback		FOOTBALL RÉSUMÉ	TWITTER FOLLOWING
2,422 career passing yards 17 career touchdown passes 173 career completions 0x Pro Bowl 0x All-Pro			**2.9MM**
Tight End			
6,095 career receiving yards 68 career touchdown catches 405 career receptions 4x Pro Bowl ('11, '12, '14, '15) 2x Super Bowl champion (XLIX, LI)	Most touchdown receptions by a TE, season: 17 ('11) Most receiving yards by a TE, season: 1,327 ('11) 3x First-team All-Pro ('11, '14, '15)		**3.3MM**
Quarterback			
66,111 career passing yards 465 career touchdown passes 5,836 career completions Super Bowl champion and MVP (XLIV) 10x Pro Bowl ('04, '06, '08–'14, '16)	First-team All-Pro ('06) 2x NFL Offensive Player of the Year ('08, '11) 7x NFL passing yards leader ('06, '08, '11, '12, '14–'16)		**2.4MM**
Cornerback			
20 career interceptions 64 career passes defensed 6x Pro Bowl ('11–'16) 3x First-team All-Pro ('11, '13, '15) NFL record 4 punt-return touchdowns, season (tied)			**372k**

Note: Player stats are from Pro-Football-Reference.com as of the 2016 season.
Twitter numbers are accurate as of September 6, 2017.

Now do the same for the below professional basketball players and the equivalent Instagram following. The answers will be on the next page, along with the names of the athletes these statistics belong to.

Guard/Forward		BASKETBALL RÉSUMÉ	INSTAGRAM FOLLOWING
12.2 points per game 1.0 assists per game 2.1 rebounds per game 0.6 steals per game 0x All-Star	0x All-NBA		**2MM**
Forward			
9.0 points per game 4.1 assists per game 6.8 rebounds per game 2x NBA champion ('15, '17) 2x NBA All-Star ('16, '17)	NBA Defensive Player of the Year ('17) 3x NBA All-Defensive First Team ('15–'17)		**2.6MM**
Forward/Center			
22.4 points per game 1.8 assists per game 10.2 rebounds per game 2.4 blocks per game 4x NBA All-Star ('14–'17)	2x All-NBA First Team ('15, '17) 2x NBA All-Defensive Second Team ('15, '17) 2x NBA blocks-per-game leader ('14, '15) NBA All-Rookie First Team ('13)		**2.2MM**
Center			
17.5 points per game 1.5 assists per game 12.7 rebounds per game 2.0 blocks per game 8x NBA All-Star ('07–'14)	5x All-NBA First Team ('09–'12) 3x NBA Defensive Player of the Year ('09–'11) 4x NBA All-Defensive First Team ('09–'12) 5x NBA rebounds-per-game leader ('08–'10, '12, '13) 2x NBA blocks-per-game leader ('09, '10)		**2.8MM**

Note: Player stats are from Basketball-Reference.com as of the 2016–2017 season. Years listed
refer to the year the season ended. Instagram numbers are accurate as of September 6, 2017.

Here are the correct pairings, along with the names of our mystery athletes.

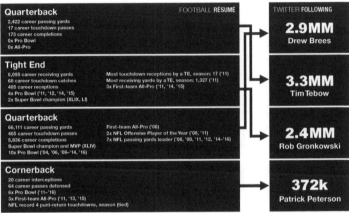

Quarterback FOOTBALL RÉSUMÉ

2,422 career passing yards
17 career touchdown passes
173 career completions
0x Pro Bowl
0x All-Pro

TWITTER FOLLOWING
2.9MM
Drew Brees

Tight End

6,095 career receiving yards
68 career touchdown catches
405 career receptions
4x Pro Bowl ('11, '12, '14, '15)
2x Super Bowl champion (XLIX, LI)

Most touchdown receptions by a TE, season: 17 ('11)
Most receiving yards by a TE, season: 1,327 ('11)
3x First-team All-Pro ('11, '14, '15)

3.3MM
Tim Tebow

Quarterback

66,111 career passing yards
465 career touchdown passes
5,836 career completions
Super Bowl champion and MVP (XLIV)
10x Pro Bowl ('04, '06, '08–'14, '16)

First-team All-Pro ('06)
2x NFL Offensive Player of the Year ('08, '11)
7x NFL passing yards leader ('06, '08, '11, '12, '14–'16)

2.4MM
Rob Gronkowski

Cornerback

20 career interceptions
64 career passes defended
6x Pro Bowl ('11–'16)
3x First-team All-Pro ('11, '13, '15)
NFL record 4 punt-return touchdowns, season (tied)

372k
Patrick Peterson

Note: Player stats are from Pro-Football-Reference.com as of the 2016 season.
Twitter numbers are accurate as of September 6, 2017.

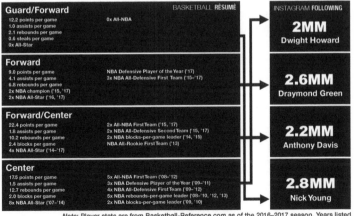

Guard/Forward BASKETBALL RÉSUMÉ

12.2 points per game
1.0 assists per game
2.1 rebounds per game
0.6 steals per game
0x All-Star

0x All-NBA

INSTAGRAM FOLLOWING
2MM
Dwight Howard

Forward

9.0 points per game
4.1 assists per game
6.8 rebounds per game
2x NBA champion ('15, '17)
2x NBA All-Star ('16, '17)

NBA Defensive Player of the Year ('17)
3x NBA All-Defensive First Team ('15–'17)

2.6MM
Draymond Green

Forward/Center

22.4 points per game
1.8 assists per game
10.2 rebounds per game
2.4 blocks per game
4x NBA All-Star ('14–'17)

2x All-NBA First Team ('15, '17)
2x NBA All-Defensive Second Team ('15, '17)
2x NBA blocks-per-game leader ('14, '15)
NBA All-Rookie First Team ('13)

2.2MM
Anthony Davis

Center

17.5 points per game
1.5 assists per game
12.7 rebounds per game
2.0 blocks per game
8x NBA All-Star ('07–'14)

5x All-NBA First Team ('08–'12)
3x NBA Defensive Player of the Year ('09–'11)
4x NBA All-Defensive First Team ('09–'12)
5x NBA rebounds-per-game leader ('08–'10, '12, '13)
2x NBA blocks-per-game leader ('09, '10)

2.8MM
Nick Young

Note: Player stats are from Basketball-Reference.com as of the 2016–2017 season. Years listed refer to the year the season ended. Instagram numbers are accurate as of September 6, 2017.

Surprised? You shouldn't be. Tim Tebow and Nick Young may not have the athletic stats to put them in their respective halls of fame, but they have brands that will keep them culturally relevant for a long time. Not only did Tim Tebow have more followers than any active player in the NFL at the point of this writing, but he also had more followers than any player in Major League Baseball. Including those of Mike Trout, Anthony Rizzo, and Bryce Harper combined. And Nick Young's brand has been long in the making—he was the subject of a documentary *before* he was in the NBA. If I were the director of marketing sitting across the table, theirs are the résumés I'd want to see.

Both are examples of "instafamous," defined by the *Huffington Post* as celebrities from platforms like "Instagram, Twitter and YouTube who are raking in fans by the millions and winning proportional paid sponsorships."

Young and Tebow each agreed to deals with adidas at points in their careers when few brands seemed willing to invest in them. Those other brands were relying on stats like passing yards and points per game to identify which athletes to sign endorsement deals with. Meanwhile, adidas had been at the forefront of the social media movement for years, putting as much emphasis on social influence as athletic performance. The lesson here is that stats do matter, but in today's world you are just as likely to earn an endorsement deal for your follower count as you are for your home run count.

"how many followers do they have?"

If you don't think followers matter as much as athletic performance, you're giving the executives across the table way too much credit. Let me give you a peek behind the curtain to put things into perspective. While at adidas, when it came time to sign a new crop of athletes, the first thing I would ask my sports marketing counterpart was, "How big is their social network?" I wanted to know how many people followed them on platforms like Twitter and Instagram. The reasoning was simple: the more people who follow a given athlete, the more people that athlete will reach with each post.

The folks you're trying to convince to bring you on as an endorser or perhaps as a full-time employee have more projects on their plates than they can handle. Every single one of them is in the midst of a time shortage. Because of that, these folks are going to look at what information is easily available to them, and there's no simpler way to measure popularity today than through social media following.

Now, I'm not saying buy bots (fake followers) that simply drive up your fan count without anyone interacting with your posts. Engagement within your community is just as important as its size. But I am suggesting that

> There's no simpler way to measure popularity today than through social media following.

you build a social media strategy that emphasizes network growth (I'll show you how in chapter 3) and that you start implementing that strategy today.

If you build it, brands will come.

Nadeshot > Julio Jones

If you don't know who Nadeshot is, don't worry; I had no idea who he is either. I was walking through the halls of adidas one day and happened to run into a colleague of mine who mentioned that he had recently sent shoes to Mr. Shot, also known as Matthew Haag. And not just any shoes. I'm talking about the NMD and Ultraboost, two of the most coveted sneakers in the industry at the time. These were the types of products reserved for the most influential figures in sports and entertainment—shoes that I myself had a hard time getting my hands on as an employee! All this for a person I had never heard of.

The joke was on me, though. It turns out Nadeshot is kind of a big deal. Haag, born in 1992 and now retired, was an eSports champion. His preferred game: *Call of Duty*. Not exactly the type of celebrity I was used to. Even more surprising was the scale of celebrity we were dealing with. At the time he received his box full of shoes, Haag had more Twitter followers (1.8 million) than Julio Jones, Jeff Gordon, Jordan Spieth, and the New York Knicks.

If you're an athlete reading this and wondering why your favorite shoe brand hasn't been sending *you* the latest sneaker drops, check the Twitter tape. How many followers do you have? Matthew Haag has 1.8 million people to thank for those shoes.

But this instafame phenomenon doesn't stop with Nadeshot. In fact, there are several digital icons out there, with more emerging every day. Whether you know their names or not, this fresh-faced group represents the future of personal branding.

That's more good news for you, because if this collection of talent can build instafame from scratch, imagine what you can do with the built-in influence and following that comes with being an athlete.

you're an influencer

The sooner you realize you're an influencer, the sooner you can start building your brand and your following. I don't care what level you're playing at; I don't even care how much success you're having. If you play sports, you're an influencer. To what degree depends on the situation you find yourself in, but the reality is there's always someone looking up to you.

If you're a varsity athlete, guess who wants to be more like *you*? Those young men or women playing on your school's junior varsity and freshman teams. If you're an NCAA athlete, guess who's looking to *you* for inspiration? Every high school athlete who dreams of playing your particular sport in college. If you're a professional athlete, why do you think people call *you* a role model? It's because what you say and do can affect the behavior and thinking of every young athlete at every level of your particular sport.

There's always someone looking up to you.

Look at the following chart to get a visual of this concept. As you move up in the sports world and subsequently up on the chart, those who have yet to reach your level (everyone south of where you sit on the diagram) become potential ambassadors for you. These are the athlete communities that you will target when building your social media following.

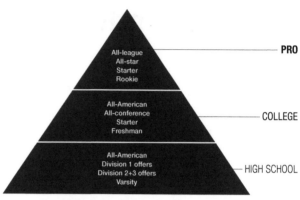

POTENTIAL **ATHLETE** AMBASSADORS

All-league All-star Starter Rookie	— **PRO**
All-American All-conference Starter Freshman	— COLLEGE
All-American Division 1 offers Division 2+3 offers Varsity	— HIGH SCHOOL

The other meaningful segment of your ambassador army comes from fans. Typically this group is made up of adults who root for your particular team and, as a result, you. As you'll see in the chart below, the fan version of our triangle has been flipped upside down. That's because as you move from high school to college to pro, the number of fans who track each level grows exponentially. More fans follow college athletes than high school athletes, and more fans follow professional athletes than college athletes.

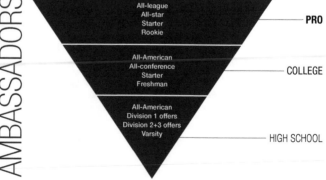

POTENTIAL **FAN** AMBASSADORS

All-league All-star Starter Rookie	— **PRO**
All-American All-conference Starter Freshman	— COLLEGE
All-American Division 1 offers Division 2+3 offers Varsity	— HIGH SCHOOL

Your potential ambassador army is the aggregate of the communities south of where you sit on both of these diagrams.

But the ultimate size of your army and the level of influence you obtain depend not just on your athletic level but also on timing and the amount of effort you give to developing and promoting your brand among these communities.

Your time is now. And your time is short.

window of influence

So I've mentioned this "window of influence" idea a couple of times, and since I love charts, I've built two to help demonstrate. The first diagram shows the time frame during which an individual can leverage his or her athletic influence to create a personal brand. Spoiler alert: it's not long.

In simple terms, if you do nothing by way of brand building, your window of influence will essentially match your athletic career. It starts the day you put on a high school uniform for the first time, and it'll close once your influence within a sport begins to decline (and it will, no matter how great you are). That influence could last through high school, college, or, for a very lucky few, the professional ranks.

Here's how the window of influence can look for an NFL athlete who plays professionally for the league average of 3.5 years. Let's call him Joe.

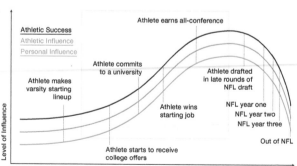

JEREMY DARLOW

As you can see, at some point Joe's athletic influence begins to decline. The problem here is that, because he hasn't built a brand that reaches beyond his sport, once his career nears its end, his personal influence follows the same negative trajectory. When his career comes to a complete close, so too do his influence and relevance. This puts Joe in the unenviable position of joining the rest of us poor saps in the working world. Yes, life becomes a never-ending cycle of building résumés, interviewing for jobs, and working for The Man. You don't want that. Trust me.

Now, here is how it *should* look for an athlete who finished his NFL career after the league average of 3.5 years but started building a personal brand well in advance. Let's call him Greg.

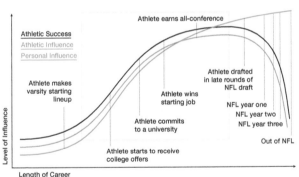

You can see the difference. First, the incline is much steeper and starts much earlier. Greg began building a brand the moment he earned his place in a starting lineup. Second, Greg reaches a much higher level of influence *because* he started sooner. Thanks to the momentum he built early on, the impact he has at every major milestone (receiving college offers, committing to a school, earning all-conference, etc.) is amplified.

Lastly, and most important, Greg's personal influence line does not fall off like Joe's did. As you can see, Greg's personal influence eventually surpasses his athletic influence. That's because personal influence acts as a combined total of the influence gained on the field *and* off.

Greg leveraged his window of athletic celebrity in order to build equity in another area of passion for him. And it's in that area where he now has a sustainable impact. He's no longer reliant on his sport to ensure success.

Don't just work for your sport—make your sport work for you.

why you need a brand

This is the point where we take a walk down memory lane to my own high school career. In those bygone days, teachers just loved to use scare tactics to keep their students from making bad decisions. Regardless of the subject, the message was always very dramatic: *If you make the wrong choice, the consequences will be severe*. Did I like the approach? Not really. It felt condescending, and I could do without the horrifying slideshows that seemed to come with every lesson. Did I get the point? Yes. What I took away from each class was that knowledge is power: by knowing the situation I'm walking into, I have a better chance of finding success and avoiding potential pitfalls.

Still, the last thing I want to do in this book is patronize you with horror story after horror story. But I would be doing you a disservice if I didn't inform you about the situation you're walking into. There are some harsh realities that come with an aspiring professional sports career, the severity of which can and will be reduced by simply being prepared. Remember, having a personal brand can be one of the most effective ways to avoid becoming a statistic.

Your chances of playing sports in college or professionally are low.

Approximately 2% of high school athletes earn athletic scholarships in college.

2%

Less than 2% of NCAA student athletes go on to become professional athletes.

PROBABILITY OF
GOING PRO
(US Only)

High school athletes
College athletes

	MLB	NFL	NHL	NBA	MLS
High school	0.6%	0.08%	0.1%	0.03%	0.04%
College	11.6%	1.7%	1.3%	1.2%	1%

Your chances of going bankrupt after a professional career are high.

78%

According to *Sports Illustrated*, 78% of NFL players go broke in their first two years out of the league.

According to *Sports Illustrated*, 60% of NBA players go broke within their first five years out of the league.

60%

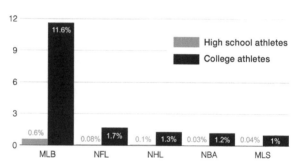

$110MM

According to Yahoo! Finance, former University of Kentucky and NBA basketball player Antoine Walker lost $110MM earned during his NBA career.

According to the *New York Times*, former professional boxer Mike Tyson was at one point $23MM in debt after earning between $300MM and $400MM during his career.

$23MM

Your financial role models are Marshawn Lynch and Rob Gronkowski.

According to *Business Insider*, after nine years in the NFL, Marshawn Lynch had yet to spend any of his $49.7MM in NFL earnings.

According to CBS Sports, after five years in the NFL, tight end Rob Gronkowski had yet to spend any of his NFL earnings.

"Marshawn Lynch has a lot of money. He hasn't spent a dime of his actual playing money . . . ever."
—Ian Rapoport, NFL Network

"I live off my marketing money and haven't blown it on any big-money expensive cars, expensive jewelry or tattoos and still wear my favorite pair of jeans from high school."
—Rob Gronkowski

Your time in the league is short.

AVERAGE CAREER LENGTH BY PRO SPORTS LEAGUE

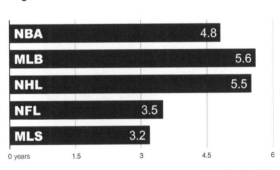

League	Years
NBA	4.8
MLB	5.6
NHL	5.5
NFL	3.5
MLS	3.2

0 years   1.5   3   4.5   6

Source: Schwartz (2013).

Your time to build a sustainable and differentiated brand is

NOW.

athletes are brands too

public service announcement

Before we move on to chapter 2, I have one more story to share. Like many of you, when I was in college I knew what I wanted to do before any of my friends. I had it in my mind that I was going to be the head of brand marketing for either adidas or Nike football. I was all in on my dream, and there wasn't anything or anyone that could get in my way.

But even with that unflinching determination and focus, I knew I needed to be ready for two potential scenarios:

- ➡ **I didn't make it.**
- ➡ **I made it but realized it wasn't a fit.**

In each case, I prepared by building a personal brand strong enough to ensure that I would land on my feet no matter what. I was maniacal about always moving forward.

In 2008, I was honored to become the head of brand marketing for adidas football and baseball. I had reached my goal. But that achievement didn't change my approach, even after leaving adidas to start my own brand consulting firm. Every day I continue to look for ways to make myself more valuable in the spaces I'm most passionate about. Every day I look for ways to build my brand.

I want the same for you. I want to encourage you to not let the statistics keep you from pursuing your dream. Let's be completely honest—the odds of making it in professional athletics are not great. In fact, they're terrible.

But the odds of becoming the head of brand marketing for football at adidas or Nike were even worse. There were literally only two people in the world who had that job, and I wanted to be one of them. I'm thankful every day that I made it.

What I ask from you is to be prepared like I was. Like I am. I ask that you look at the 78 percent of NFL and the 60 percent of NBA athletes who have gone bankrupt since their careers have ended and not say, "That won't be me" based purely on how far you can throw a football or how well you can dribble a basketball. Instead, look at the stats and say, "That won't be me" because you're prepared whether you make it to the league or not. Because you've used the celebrity afforded you by way of your athletic talent to build a brand that keeps your personal life moving forward.

if now, how?

So the question is, how? How does one build a personal brand? The rest of this book is dedicated to lessons and strategies that will help you develop your brand. The most important is to create a brand positioning statement—a single sentence that reflects the space you hope to occupy in people's minds. This statement will represent who you are and what sets you apart from the competition.

This is your moment—right now, as you read this book. This is the moment when you decide to take your destiny into your own hands. This is the moment you realize that athletes are brands too. And more importantly, this is the moment when, together, we start building your brand.

CH**1** YOUR INFLUENCE

THE INTERNET IS THE NEW PLACE FOR

OVERNIGHT STARDOM.

—HUFFINGTON POST

KIM
KARDASHIAN WEST
HAS **101MM**
INSTAGRAM FOLLOWERS

MORE THAN:
LEBRON JAMES
SERENA WILLIAMS
TOM BRADY

TIM
TEBOW
HAS **3.3MM**
TWITTER FOLLOWERS

MORE THAN:
DREW BREES
ROB GRONKOWSKI
PATRICK PETERSON

NADESHOT
HAS **1.8MM**
TWITTER FOLLOWERS

MORE THAN:
JULIO JONES
JEFF GORDON
THE NY KNICKS

SOCIAL MEDIA HAS GIVEN
POWER TO THE PEOPLE.

YOU'RE AN INFLUENCER

HOW **INFLUENTIAL** IS UP TO YOU

JEREMY DARLOW

YOUR WINDOW OF INFLUENCE:

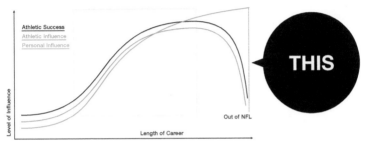

Athletic Success
Athletic Influence
Personal Influence

Level of Influence

Out of NFL

Length of Career

THIS

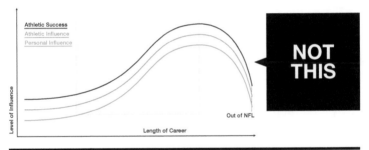

Athletic Success
Athletic Influence
Personal Influence

Level of Influence

Out of NFL

Length of Career

NOT THIS

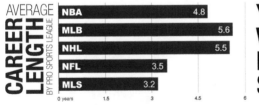

AVERAGE
CAREER LENGTH BY PRO SPORTS LEAGUE

NBA	4.8
MLB	5.6
NHL	5.5
NFL	3.5
MLS	3.2

0 years   1.5   3   4.5   6

YOUR WINDOW IS SMALL.

YOUR TIME IS NOW.

Approximately 2% of high school athletes earn athletic scholarships in college.

 2%

Less than 2% of NCAA student athletes go on to become professional athletes.

2

your
brand

more than an athlete

On August 1, 2016, I learned that it's not just athletes who aren't prepared to build a brand—it's the people surrounding them. Even more alarming was the discovery that many of those people are actually *against* the idea of athletes building personal brands.

On that summer day, the NCAA implemented a new rule in college athletics that, for the first time, allowed university coaches to publicly engage with (like, retweet, favorite, and share) the social media posts of the high school athletes that they were recruiting. The next twenty-four hours were a bit of a free-for-all as coaches began retweeting and liking in droves. One sports news network put together a chart representing the number of times Southeastern Conference (SEC) football coaches had retweeted potential recruits' posts after one day of the new rule. Butch Jones, head coach of the University of Tennessee, had done so 108 times, more than any other coach in the conference. Both the social media and recruiting games had officially changed.

I looked at the new rule along with those numbers and immediately saw the exposure opportunity suddenly available to the high school athlete. In response, I tweeted a photo of the ESPN chart along with the following:

> Real winners of new recruiting rule are HS [high school] athlete brands. Social exposure 📈 📈 📈 #AthletesAreBrandsToo

Boy, did that rub some people the wrong way. That night I got into my first ever Twitter fight.

The response that sparked the debate came from an individual who claimed in his Twitter profile to actually work for one of the major recruiting sites. I don't think he liked what I had to say.

I've legit seen some awful tweets since I got into this game but, my God, is this one of the worst of the bunch.

He continued:

And people have criticized hoops recruiting for years, now we're promoting "HS athlete brands"…what a joke.

I started to get a tad disturbed by this gentleman's commentary. But I kept my cool on Twitter, because, you know, the brand. I also knew that this was exactly the point of view I needed to hear before writing a book on the subject. So I prodded a bit:

Appreciate the passion—why is it bad for athletes to improve their brand? Important for everyone, no?

I nudged a couple more times:

More successful young men/women are at building a pers brand, more likely they are to succeed post athletics. Why is that bad?

Very few of these athletes will make it to the professional levels, even then, there are no guarantees. Need to prep for post sport career.

That's when some others started to chime in. Apparently, I was (and maybe still am, for these people) the worst:

@JeremyDarlow Fan of yours typically, but this is off-base. How (actually; not theoretically) does one RT [retweet] help w/ post-sport career?

At this point my hair was standing on end (more than usual) from the shock. How could people be so oblivious to personal branding and, in this case, the power of social media?

To answer that last tweeter's question, here's why it matters. One single retweet from an SEC football coach can provide a young man with additional exposure to

- ➡ **football coaches and programs that follow the coach,**
- ➡ **football media that follow the coach,**
- ➡ **football influencers that follow the coach, and**
- ➡ **football fans that follow the coach.**

Furthermore, coaches are themselves influencers who have the ability to validate an athlete's skill set with a single public endorsement—which a retweet absolutely is. So if we're keeping score, that "one RT" can drive brand awareness among coaches, football programs, media, and fans across the country. That "one RT" also helps grow an athlete's number of followers, which can only help improve his chances at a scholarship, not to mention aid in positioning him as an influencer himself.

Finally, an athlete that a head coach at an SEC program deems worthy enough to retweet is more than likely being recruited by several other prominent head coaches—all of whom will see their competition publicly engaging with the young man. And, as we now know, retweets lead to more retweets.

Meanwhile, my original detractor, the one who worked for the recruiting service? Yeah, he wasn't having it:

@JeremyDarlow Dude, stop.

Then came this response from, according to his Twitter profile, an "NBA Draft Analyst":

@JeremyDarlow No, that's how you end up with college athletes, potential pros, worrying about wrong things

To which I replied:

When we consider our extracurricular activities and GPA in high school to get academic schollies, that's brand mkt

We'd be negligent if we didn't encourage athletes to build their brands in the same way we encourage other students to build theirs for entrance to college and "the real world." Let's be honest: most high school students don't participate in extracurricular activities for love of debate or French or the saxophone (and a comparative hatred of free time spent watching TV and hanging out with friends). It's about looking good on a college application—in other words, the brand.

What baffles me is that these so-called overachievers are encouraged to build a well-rounded body of work that stands out among the competition, yet when it comes to the six-foot-five high school football player with a rocket for an arm, we encourage "focus." Everything else is suddenly considered a distraction. What's the difference? Why do we treat athletes differently from nonathlete students?

I followed up on Twitter with this:

> Just because a young man/woman is an athlete, doesn't stop the need for a brand. Need to prepare everyone for post athletics.

Our instigator friend appeared to have had enough:

> @JeremyDarlow I'm done with you, man. You're going to do your thing regardless, we can agree to disagree.

Needless to say, I don't expect this individual to attend any of the book signings.

For the athletes, parents, and coaches reading this, know that there will always be those who refuse to see a world beyond athletics, people who will tell you to put all your eggs in one basket.

But athletes who fail to reach the professional ranks do so not because they spent too much time building a résumé or personal brand. In fact, it's quite the opposite. According to the NCAA, "student-athletes graduate at a higher rate than the general student body." Focus is not the problem. Athletes fail to reach the professional ranks because it's hard!

If less than 2 percent of NCAA athletes go on to play professional sports, how can we as a society not properly prepare them, beginning in high school, for a life post-sport? How can we not encourage these individuals to start building a brand while they have influence? This isn't about taking time away from athletics and skill development on the field or golf course. This is about building a brand armed with a résumé relevant to the world that exists off it.

So that's what I'm going to do: teach you how to position your personal brand in a way that differentiates you from the competition and increases your chances of post-athletics success.

Starting with your story.

a brand name to remember

Great brands start with great stories, and great stories leave a lasting impression.

You may not know the school Michael Oher attended or the teams he played for in the NFL, but you no doubt recognize his story. It's one made famous by *The Blind Side*, a book and major motion picture that chronicle Oher's journey from homelessness to professional football. It's a story that earned actress Sandra Bullock an Oscar and author Michael Lewis national acclaim. More importantly, it's a tale that has almost certainly guaranteed the permanence of Oher's name. The offensive lineman from the state of Mississippi is unlikely to finish as one of the greatest ever to play the game of football, but because of his incredible story and the inner workings of the human brain, the name Michael Oher will be remembered well after his career ends.

According to an article in *Fast Company*, our memories thrive off storytelling, saying, "It's far easier for us to remember stories than the cold hard facts." This claim is supported by a study conducted by Jennifer Aaker, a marketing professor at the Stanford Graduate School of Business. In the study, Aaker's

Great brands start with great stories.

students were asked to give a one-minute pitch to their classmates. Those in the audience were asked to write down what they remembered from each presentation. The results speak to the power of storytelling, as only 5 percent of the class recalled a statistic, while 63 percent remembered the story.

Stories drive recall, making them critical to building any successful brand, whether it's for a product, a service, a team, or in our case, a person. The most successful marketers in the world are also not coincidentally the best storytellers. They know that even the most brilliantly designed product alone is not enough. It's how you present that product that creates demand and brings people back.

The better your story, the stronger your brand.

black cards are for rich people

The American Express Centurion, commonly known as simply "the Amex black card," is a titanium credit card that has become synonymous with affluence. *Forbes* called it "the Bugatti of credit cards." Yahoo! Finance described it as the "status symbol du jour for high-end cardholders." If you have one, you're part of a very elite community and no doubt get excited every time you have a reason to pull it out of your wallet.

The reality is, the card itself is not much different from any other credit card, and it actually charges higher fees than some of its competitors. But for black-card holders, none of that matters. What does matter is the status that comes with it—status built from a calculated story spun by some very intelligent marketers at American Express. From the deluxe presentation upon arrival to your home or office to the color black itself, the product exudes superiority and sophistication. *(Note that the following positioning statements are my projections and words not those of the person or brand.)*

The black card is the credit card for the 1%.

Jay-Z is a business, man

Despite his notoriously humble beginnings, Shawn "Jay-Z" Carter may have built the personal brand that most closely resembles the Amex black card, one that brings to mind a slew of lavish buzzwords: *exclusivity*, *prosperity*, *luxury*, and *business*. Taking advice from the likes of billionaire mogul Warren Buffett, Carter has become hip-hop's CEO, transforming his brand unlike anyone before or since.

> ❝ Most times rappers end up broke or nowhere. It's time for someone to take it to the next level, to become an executive and open the doors for the culture. ❞ Jay-Z

Is he the first hip-hop artist to make it out of a tough environment? Absolutely not. But he's one of the first to successfully transition from the streets to the recording studio to the boardroom. Carter was never going to be just a rapper. From the beginning, he had his eyes set on something more, and he wove that narrative into everything he did, which he expressed perfectly in the remix of "Diamonds from Sierra Leone," when he describes himself not as a businessman but rather a business in his own right. After reportedly selling over 55 million albums over the course of his career, it's

athletes are brands too

hard to argue with him. From the cars he drives to the clothes he wears, Carter's brand never wavers. There is only one Shawn Carter story, and it's a carefully crafted one.

BRAND POSITIONING STATEMENT
Jay-Z is hip-hop's CEO.

John Urschel is smart AF

How is it that an offensive lineman drafted in the fifth round, who started just thirteen of his first forty games while earning zero NFL Pro Bowl selections, found himself featured in two nationally televised commercials? One was alongside three-time NFL Defensive Player of the Year J. J. Watt. How does that happen? Storytelling. John Urschel's story is unlike anything you've seen from a professional football player, and because of that, fans, journalists, and sponsors can't get enough.

Urschel's story is of an athlete with an intellect so rare that it transcends sports. His television appearances have little to do with his ability to protect the quarterback or open holes for a running back; they have everything to do with the bachelor's and master's degrees in mathematics that he earned while playing football at Penn State. Not to mention the William V. Campbell Trophy, also known as the "Academic Heisman," that he earned while in college. Oh, and his unexpected celebrity status almost certainly has something to do with his pursuance of a PhD in mathematics from MIT, one of the most respected schools for mathematics in the world—all while playing professional football. Urschel has made such a name for himself that in 2017, *Forbes* named him to their "30 Under 30" list celebrating outstanding young scientists.

> **❝ I plan to be a great mathematician. ❞** John Urschel

There is perhaps no better example of an athlete using his athletic influence and platform to build notoriety around a personal brand. Is he the first scholar to play football? Not by a long shot; Stanford, Duke, Michigan, and many more college football programs can attest to that. But he's one of the first to write a story that leads with academia, not athletics. Urschel's story is not of a football player who happens to be an intellectual. Urschel's story is of an intellectual who happened to play football. And it's for that reason that Urschel's brand is in demand.

BRAND POSITIONING STATEMENT

John Urschel is football's mathematician.

what's your story?

It should be clear now that personal brands are nothing more than strategically constructed stories of which you, the athlete, are the author. That might sound like an intimidating spot to be in for someone without much marketing experience, but the writing process is not as complicated as it may seem. In fact, it's made up of just two steps, starting with research and ending with your positioning statement. I'm about to break down both of these to their simplest elements.

Before I do, let's talk about effort. The prominence of your brand will directly correlate to the amount of energy you put into the process. Jay-Z didn't graduate from the streets of Brooklyn by chance. He became an entertainment mogul because of the hours he spent locked in his room perfecting his craft. It's no accident that John Urschel landed two television commercials; it has everything to do with the fact that he read about mathematics during his free time while traveling to NFL road games. I tell every young marketer I work with the same thing: some marketers are born with a natural instinct for the industry, but the greatest marketers of our generation just wanted it more.

> **❝ Nothing will work unless you do. ❞**
> John Wooden, UCLA basketball coach, 1948–1975

Let's get started.

step 1:
situation analysis

The most important element of any marketing plan is the brand positioning statement. This statement will become the mantra you use to crystalize what makes your brand unique while guiding everything you do from this point on. Whether you're working with endorsers or philanthropies, giving a postgame interview or posting a photo to Instagram, every element of your life going forward will contribute to establishing your brand as the entity you describe in this statement. But before you write it, you need to understand it.

The central process through which a statement is determined is called a *situation analysis*. This is where you separate good brands from great brands. In his book *A New Brand World*, author and renowned marketer Scott Bedbury calls this practice the "big dig," in which you as the developer of the marketing plan pull together research ranging from industry trends to personal history, competitive analysis to personality traits. Your goal is to figure out where you fit within the landscape of athletes and influencers around you.

Take the filter off—nothing is off-limits. If you think it's interesting and even remotely applicable to your brand, write it down. Other brands that you find

> **The most important element of any marketing plan is the brand positioning statement.**

compelling? Write them down. Athletes whose post-sports careers inspire you? Write them down. What tools are other athletes using to reach followers? What are the things they do that attract attention? What trends are you seeing in the sport you play?

Not only is this a chance to become knowledgeable about what's happening in the world around you, but this is your opportunity to look inside and discover what truly motivates you, what makes you special, and what makes you happy. It's an introspective deep dive. When you think you've exhausted your exploration, you should be left with what feels like an overwhelming amount of research. That's what we want.

Here are a few places to start your analysis.

look in the mirror

People often assume that athletes are only passionate about the sport they play, but that's rarely the case. In many instances, an individual's natural physical talent sets them up for success in the pool or on the diamond, but outside of athletics is where they truly find their greatest inspiration. For your brand to be successful, it must be built on a foundation of passion. Part of your personal discovery will be to uncover that which brings you to life.

> **❝** As much as I love basketball, my whole life I've been passionate about other things too. **❞** Damian Lillard

First-round pick. Rookie of the year. All-star. Rapper. Damian Lillard is more than an NBA player; he's also a musician, and a good one at that. Dame DOLLA, as he is known in the music world, has earned every bit of respect he's garnered outside of the NBA. In 2013 he started "4BarFriday," a weekly Instagram freestyle challenge that has over 65,000 followers. Lillard leveraged his athletic celebrity to open the door to a promising music career. According to renowned radio host Sway Calloway, the Portland Trail Blazer has turned his passion into a potential full-time vocation and brand differentiator: "Damian Lillard is the best rapper in the NBA."

BRAND POSITIONING STATEMENT

Damian Lillard is the athlete fusing basketball and hip-hop.

Ask yourself:

➡ **What do I love?**
➡ **What is it that gets me out of bed?**
➡ **If I weren't playing sports, what would I be doing? Why?**

look at them

You can't differentiate your brand without knowing what personalities and characters currently exist within your respective industry. The quickest way to break through the clutter is to establish a story unlike anything your audience has seen before. In order for that to happen, you must understand your competition inside and out. The more you know about your rivals, the easier it will be to separate yourself from them.

> **❝** Maybe I don't look like the average punter, but that's cool with me, because I'm not trying to be average. **❞**
> Marquette King

You might not recognize the name Marquette King, but chances are you'd know the name if I preceded it with "the dancing punter." In fact, if you type "dancing punter" into Google, you'll find yourself inundated with story after story about the NFL's most charismatic specialist who has become known more for his theatrics after the kick than for the kick itself. In a league overcome by sack and touchdown dances, how is it that Marquette King's dancing stands out? It's because he's a punter, and punters don't dance, at least none that I've seen. King found and exploited a void within his own particular profession. While every other player on the field—even the kicker—could be found celebrating and showing off his personality at times throughout a game, for whatever reason, punters could not. Until King. It's because of that stereotype-defying approach that we know who he is.

BRAND POSITIONING STATEMENT

Marquette King is the punter with personality.

Ask yourself:

➡ **What is the competition doing to stand out and make a name for themselves?**
➡ **What is missing in my profession? How can I make a name for myself?**
➡ **Are there stereotypes associated with my sport or position? Can I break them?**

look at the time

Often the state of a sport and the cultural context in which an athlete plays provides a platform to build a differentiated brand. Timing can be as important as the brand itself. Look at the athletic and cultural landscape you find yourself in and ask yourself if there are shifts happening that your brand can leverage.

> **ff** Joe came at the time he was destined to come. **JJ** John Dockery, a former teammate of Joe Namath

In 1969, Baltimore Colts quarterback Johnny Unitas, described by the *New York Times* as "reticent, workmanlike and deliberately unglamorous," was the poster child for the old NFL and the old America. Respectful, humble, and unassuming (as exemplified by his signature crew cut), Unitas in many ways represented the establishment. Meanwhile in New York stood Joe Namath, who, in direct contrast, represented a developing antiestablishment movement. Namath was all about glitz and glamour, and that's why it worked—he was the flashy icon that the younger, more rebellious generation was looking for. Broadway Joe was able to personify a cultural shift, and his personality aligned perfectly with the era in which he played. Namath was the right athlete at the right time, and it's for that reason he remains a legend in the sport.

*Joe Namath was a superstar
on and off the field.*

Ask yourself:

➡ **Is my sport evolving? How can I become a face of that change?**
➡ **Is society looking for a fresh voice in an area I am passionate about?**
➡ **How can I use my athletic platform to align myself with the movement?**

step 2:
positioning statement

Trust me when I say the hard part is over. All of your research is about to pay off in the form of a carefully crafted positioning statement. Before you begin writing your statement, it's important to understand its structure. I like to break it down into two parts:

1. The **frame of reference:** the landscape in which you are comparing yourself.
2. The **point of differentiation:** your brand differentiator.

For example, a positioning statement for someone like Super Bowl–winning quarterback Russell Wilson might break down like this:

FRAME OF REFERENCE: *The professional football player...*

POINT OF DIFFERENTIATION: *...who is a role model on and off the field.*

Wilson's frame of reference is broader than most, covering the entire National Football League's roster of athletes. The scale of his reference point is based on the elite stature of Wilson's personal brand and the success he's achieved in his career. For others who have yet to reach his level, a more focused frame of reference is appropriate. That might mean concentrating on a specific position ("The professional quarterback...") or even further narrowing to within a conference or division ("The professional quarterback from the NFC West..."). Start with a narrow frame of reference and broaden it as you grow your brand.

Wilson's point of differentiation, on the other hand, is based entirely on his own day-to-day behavior and brand positioning aspirations. The former Wisconsin Badger is consistently striving to make a difference in the lives of children in his community. Giving back is genuinely part of who Wilson is, and it's reflected in the brand he portrays to the public. As a result, that generosity is also reflected in his ultimate positioning statement.

After combining Wilson's frame of reference with his point of differentiation, the All-Pro quarterback's brand position looks something like this:

Russell Wilson is a role model on and off the football field.

Now, you are obviously not Russell Wilson, and this is of course not your brand's statement. But there are lessons to be learned from this execution and others that will help guide you through the writing process.

be authentic

A crucial element of any successful brand is authenticity. If your statement is not aligned with your own personal values, how long do you think it will last? If you don't believe in the story you're telling, no one will. Coaches, fans, and the media will see through your attempt to be something you're not.

Be true to yourself. Take pride in what makes you unique. People follow leaders, and leaders don't follow anyone. Carve your own path.

❝ Today you are you, that is truer than true. There is no one alive who is Youer than You. **❞** Dr. Seuss

kill indifference

"Kill indifference" is a brand-marketing mantra I live by every day. In order for your brand to be successful, you need to elicit reactions; if people are indifferent about your brand, you've failed. The hang-up here is that people typically want to be accepted and liked. That opens the door for the brave few willing to risk a negative response, as most are reluctant to take chances with their brand. Bad for them, good for you. It's not a brand's job to make everyone happy. Rather, a brand's job is to make a *portion* of the population *very* happy. Be yourself, no matter what.

> **❝ People either love me or hate me. ❞**
> Brian Bosworth

Brian Bosworth, former University of Oklahoma and Seattle Seahawks linebacker, has to be one of the most polarizing figures in the history of sport. And as a marketer, I love him for it. Bosworth killed indifference as well as any athlete I've ever seen. Often prone to speaking in the third person, the man himself had this to say about, well, himself: "The Boz is highly controversial, highly sensational." He would go on to call himself an "extremist." From his rebellious haircut, referred to as "the Boz cut" by the

media, to the signature sunglasses he wore during interviews, Bosworth had a personal brand before most athletes knew what it meant. "I never met an athlete who could market himself better," said Rick Reilly, coauthor of the book *The Boz*. On the field, The Boz was a magnet for controversy; off the field, he was just as provocative. In the words of University of Oklahoma teammate Spencer Tillman: "He was creating the latitude to leverage his brand in a way that brought him value beyond the football field." The key words here being "beyond the football field."

Thirty years later, despite what many considered to be a disappointing career in the NFL, companies are still paying The Boz to endorse their products thanks to the provocative brand he built off the field.

BRAND POSITIONING STATEMENT
*Brian Bosworth was a rebel
on and off the field.*

say it with confidence

A colleague of mine once said, "If you say it with confidence, it's true." He was right. Like it or not, we live in a world where charisma often supersedes understanding and style can overtake substance. As a result it's not what you say, it's *how* you say it. As it relates to athletes, I'd dare to say it's not how many shots you make, it's how you make them. It's not who you tackle, it's how hard you tackle them. And it's not how many home runs you hit, it's how far you hit them. People like steak, but they love sizzle. Give them both.

> **❝ It's hard to be humble when you're as great as I am. ❞** Muhammad Ali

Perhaps the preeminent showman of our time, regardless of sport, Muhammad Ali once famously boasted, "I'm young; I'm handsome; I'm fast. I can't possibly be beat." Supreme confidence. That's why, even after his passing, we adore him. That's also why many opponents hated to fight him. Ali once claimed, "I am the greatest. I said that even before I knew I was." Unrivaled self-assurance. That's why we believed him. Despite the fact that he retired with fewer wins and more losses than fellow heavyweight boxing idol Joe Louis, in the minds of those who know his story, Ali will always be the greatest—like he told us.

BRAND POSITIONING STATEMENT

Muhammad Ali is the greatest boxer of all time.

stand out

Marketing author Seth Godin said it best in his celebrated book *Purple Cow*: you're either remarkable or invisible. The idea is simple, as is the choice. In a world filled with homogeny and repetitiveness (your average herd of cows), it's the brands that choose to stand out (the purple cows) that succeed.

athletes are brands too

As you construct your positioning statement, look for spaces in the market that afford you the use of differentiating words like *best*, *first*, or *only*. It is in each of these cases that your brand will achieve the strongest sense of ownership.

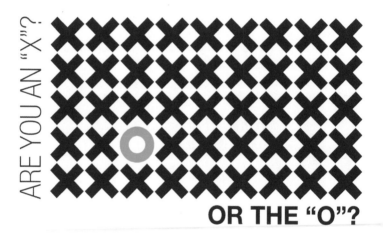

be the *best*

Bo Jackson's career didn't last long enough for him to be considered one of the greatest running backs or outfielders of our generation. It's the fact that his legacy spans multiple sports that differentiates his brand. Jackson played both professional football and baseball, and while several athletes have played more than one sport, no one did it better than Jackson. As the first athlete to be named to the All-Star Game of two sports, Jackson was chosen as the greatest athlete of all time by ESPN.

> **❝ I was the toughest SOB on the field, it didn't matter what it was. ❞** Bo Jackson

Jackson's immortalization was aided by a marketing campaign that perfectly encapsulated his enormousness. Nike's "Bo Knows" campaign told the story of an athlete who could do it all. From basketball to tennis, hockey to music, the infamous television spot suggested that the multitalented competitor could conquer anything—a story validated by his performance on the field. The commercial itself gave Jackson the perfect brand narrative and will go down as one of the finest athlete endorsement campaigns of our generation. He may not have been the first or the only multisport athlete, but there's little doubt that he was the *best*.

BRAND POSITIONING STATEMENT

Bo Jackson is the best multisport athlete of all time.

be the *first*

Danica Patrick's impact on the sport of racing has less to do with her success on the track and more to do with her being the first woman to race full-time in NASCAR's Sprint Cup series. Regardless of where her athletic career takes her, Patrick will always be seen as a pioneer for female athletes.

> **"** Something that makes you the most different compared to everyone else perhaps is also what makes your most special attribute. **"** Danica Patrick

The shards of ceiling glass she's left in her tracks have translated into a reported net worth of over $60 million, thanks in part to high-profile endorsement deals from the likes of GoDaddy and Nationwide Insurance. Patrick has written the playbook on being first, one that can be followed by other women looking to break new ground in sports.

BRAND POSITIONING STATEMENT

Danica Patrick is the first woman to race full-time in NASCAR's Sprint Cup series.

be the *only*

In the 1960s a high jumper from Oregon State University revolutionized his sport by failing. As was the case for most high jumpers in those days, Dick Fosbury was urged to use the "straddle" technique, where the jumper crosses the bar facedown. But he failed to pick up this traditional method, so instead he tried a different approach: crossing the bar faceup, which people described as going "backwards over the bar." At the time he was the *only* athlete using this method.

> **❝** In 1968 Mexico, the spectators were so surprised by what I was doing, that they stopped cheering and just looked. **❞** Dick Fosbury

Fifty years later, this preeminent technique is now known as the "Fosbury Flop." Fosbury used it to win a 1968 Olympic gold medal—along with the preservation of his brand and name forever.

BRAND POSITIONING STATEMENT

Dick Fosbury was the only high jumper to go backwards over the bar.

Ask yourself:

➡ **What can I realistically become the best at?**
➡ **Can I be the first to do something in my sport or area of passion?**
➡ **Am I doing something no one else is doing?**

find focus

Brand positioning is about focus. Pick one thing that's genuine and authentic to who you are and own it. There may be no better example of an athlete choosing to focus his efforts on one area than boxing legend Evander Holyfield. Holyfield credits his mother's advice for his success in the ring. When he was a child, Holyfield's mother told him, "You can't be great at everything. Find one thing and be the very best." Holyfield took those words to heart and finished his career as one of the greatest fighters of his generation. Follow that same advice as you develop your positioning statement. Pick one thing and be the best at it.

> **❝** If you chase two rabbits, you will not catch either one. **❞** Russian proverb

always be branding

In order for your positioning statement to resonate with your audience, you must live by your brand guidelines twenty-four hours a day. That means both on and off the court (or field or track). If your position and persona are completely based on your in-game performance, what are you left with when you can no longer play that sport? Nothing. However, if for the duration of your athletic career you have represented yourself and your brand consistently in all arenas of life, when you walk away from the game, your brand stays intact.

> **❝** Your image isn't your character. Character is what you are as a person. **❞** Derek Jeter

Derek Jeter sits at the top of the list when it comes to class and professionalism. How do I know? His peers and colleagues said so. In a poll taken by MLB.com in which former players and media members were asked to give one word to describe the man known as "The Captain," over 25 percent replied with "class," "classy," "professional," or "professionalism." That's an incredible number that demonstrates the consistently high character Jeter portrayed on and off the field.

WHICH SEQUENCE IS EASIER TO REMEMBER?

By presenting the same brand story over and over again, your audience is more likely to remember your message.

Be consistent in telling one focused story. Do that and you'll not only own a unique position among your competition, but you'll do it with less effort, less stress, and less money. By establishing a strategic and authentic positioning statement, you're setting yourself up to communicate a single, succinct message. This is who you are. This is what you stand for. This is why we should care.

Okay, *now* it's time for you to write your story:

FRAME OF REFERENCE:

POINT OF DIFFERENTIATION:

BRAND POSITIONING STATEMENT:

Now that you have your positioning statement, the next and final step is to share it with the world. The rest of this book outlines how you can create constant conversation around what makes you and your personal brand unique. This is where the real fun begins.

GREAT BRANDS START WITH GREAT STORIES:

| **BLACK CARD** THE CREDIT CARD FOR THE 1% | **JAY-Z** HIP-HOP'S CEO | **JOHN URSCHEL** FOOTBALL'S MATHEMATICIAN |

AND GREAT STORIES
ARE BUILT IN TWO STEPS:

①
SITUATION ANALYSIS
IDENTIFY THE OPPORTUNITY

②
POSITIONING STATEMENT
DEFINE YOUR PLACE IN THE MARKET

DO YOUR RESEARCH

LOOK IN
THE MIRROR
WHO ARE
YOU

LOOK AT
THEM
WHO ARE
THEY

LOOK AT
THE TIME
IS THIS YOUR
MOMENT

BE AUTHENTIC

MAKE THEM
FEEL YOU

SAY IT WITH
CONFIDENCE

STAND OUT

PICK A LANE

CHOOSE ONE POSITION AND **OWN** IT.

3

your
voice

Pee-wee Herman and Kanye West

Growing up as a kid, I remember watching a show called *Pee-wee's Playhouse*. The series first aired in 1986 and starred Paul Reubens as Pee-wee Herman. In the show Pee-wee had an aluminum foil ball. Basically it was just as it sounds: a ball of foil. One key distinction made it memorable: It. Was. Huge. Pee-wee would constantly add to it thanks to donations from his friends. The ball became so big that it could no longer fit in the play-house, so it was donated to a foil museum (apparently that's a thing).

Silly as it sounds, this ball of foil reinforces a marketing philosophy I practice and preach in my own work and one that will guide us through this section. Consistency and frequency can take what was once an overlooked idea and turn it into something people can't help but notice. Your brand is no different than this ball of foil. At first it's a standard, commonplace piece of aluminum. No one cares. Then it's little more than a wad of foil, what looks to be trash. If you saw it, you might register its existence, but more than likely you'd forget about it. But as more and more aluminum is added, the more interesting it becomes. It's not just a single piece of foil. It's not just a wad of foil. Suddenly it's a *ball* of foil. Now people are noticing. But it doesn't stop there. More and more foil is added still. Now it's not just a foil ball, it's the world's *largest* foil ball. It's unlike anything you've ever seen, and everyone wants to see it, touch it, and roll it.

Now people are talking about it. Now it's a brand people care about.

Your brand is no different than this ball of foil. Once you establish your positioning statement (the aluminum foil ball), it's about telling the same consistent story (adding foil) with frequency (a *lot* of foil). Meaning, tell people who you are and what makes you special over and over…and over again.

CONSISTENCY
+ FREQUENCY

BRAND RECALL

Which brings us to Kanye West. West will be the first to tell you he's a genius. Now that might rub you the wrong way, but that's exactly why he's right. His brilliance comes from his ability to provoke and incite reactions among his audience and the media alike. When you hear the name Kanye West, chances are you truly feel something. In many cases, it's either love or hate; what other artist elicits such an intense response? It's that ability to activate our senses along with his genuinely groundbreaking contributions to the music and fashion worlds that have many believing him when he says, "I am Warhol. I am the No. 1 most impactful artist of our generation. I am Shakespeare in the flesh." The thing that West understands perhaps better than anyone is that if you say something long enough, people start to believe you and say it back. For that he *is* a genius, whether you like him or not.

Having led the marketing efforts behind the first Yeezy football cleat, I can tell you from experience that every decision made around West's personal brand is calculated and strategic. From the shoebox to the shoelaces, nothing with his name on it leaves the building without thought and care. It's that level of detail that has led to his products selling out within minutes. That brings us to our goal in this section: to create the same level of fervor around your brand that West has around his. I'll outline how you can build a tactical communication plan that keeps your audience begging for more.

This is the last phase of our brand-marketing journey; it's about building hype and having fun. Enjoy.

draw a map

Before we jump into brand communication tactics, let's take a minute to draw your map to success. The first step toward building a successful communication strategy is to define your goals. Go into every year with a new set of objectives that, if accomplished, will contribute to your brand position. Pick three things, write them down, and tape them up on your mirror as a reminder every morning. It will be the combination of your positioning statement and these targets that guides your marketing efforts and decision making for the next twelve months.

Before you start posting on Instagram, before you tweet for the first time, before you send your first snap, define your objectives and draw a map. As I always preach to my marketing team and clients, I can't tell you how to get somewhere until you know where you want to go.

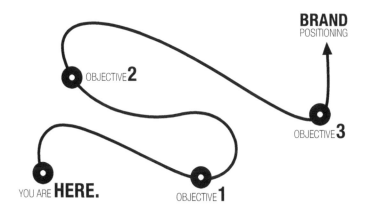

Here are three brand-marketing objectives, generalized for the sake of your own implementation, that I've used consistently over my career:

➡ **Build equity and awareness around (insert visual brand identifier).**
➡ **Be the most talked-about brand among (insert competitive set) for the year.**
➡ **Be the most talked-about brand during (insert moment or event).**

We'll walk through each of these objectives and use them as the map to your own communication strategy, beginning with your visual identity.

objective #1:
build a visual identity

In simple terms, "visual identity" encompasses any element of a brand that people can see (or envision) and ultimately use to recognize the entity. In the corporate world, that can include things like a logo, color palette, and typeface. A brand will use these features to identify and differentiate itself among its competition.

Philosophically, a personal brand is no different. However, in your case brand identity will also involve those physical elements you were born with, including hair, height, and eye color, as well as those developed and honed along the way, like clothing, car choice, and even hand gestures.

In the world of brand marketing, visual identity is critical. In life, it's just as relevant. Imagine a world free of branding. As much as we can come to hate it, not having those visual cues that we use to make decisions every day would make our lives quite difficult. Without brand identity there would be no way to know if that box of cereal you picked out was packed with your favorite kind of shredded wheat or if that sports drink was filled with Gatorade or Powerade. It would be as if you wore a blindfold to the grocery store.

Similarly, without brand identity, there would be no brand loyalty. By neglecting to give people consistent brand identifiers that will bring them back, it is nearly impossible to build a passionate following. It's those follow-ings that successful brands are built on.

Your first objective is to use what you were born with and what you can develop over time to build a visual identity that brings people back, starting with your physical appearance.

what do you look like?

A key to brand retention and differentiation is visual recognition. If you want people to remember you, your appearance matters. When people see your brand, do they distinguish it as yours? When people see you on television or in a game, do they know that it's you? Does your physical presentation differentiate you from the competition? And how does your appearance contribute to your overall positioning strategy? According to a study by 3M (the Post-it Note company), "visuals are processed 60,000 times faster than text." As a species we tend to retain information first and foremost through our eyes, making it imperative for any athlete reading this to create a unique look worth remembering.

60,000x
according to a study by 3M, "visuals are processed 60,000 times faster than text."

if you got it, flaunt it

Snowboarding great Shaun White may not have the same long, flowing hair he did as an early twentysomething winning gold at the 2006 Olympic Games in Turin, Italy, but there's no doubt the visual of his bright-red mane contributed to his present-day brand recognition. For snowboarding, a sport short on notoriety and publicity, it takes more than success to capture the attention of the masses (and with it, big-ticket sponsors). White had the professional achievements, but perhaps just as important, he also had a unique appearance. If you didn't know his name, you knew his look. Whether he wants to be known as "The Flying Tomato" today or not, there's little doubt that his hair helped him become a household name. How else can you explain the national headlines he made when he finally cut his famous locks?

if you don't got it, grow it

While Shaun White was born with his iconic red hair, others have had to manufacture that visual differentiator later on in life, including NBA all-star James Harden. According to Harden, he wouldn't shave his beard for $1 million, and that's probably a good business decision. Harden's iconic beard no doubt contributed to his 2015 mega-sponsorship deal with adidas worth $200 million. Adidas's global basketball general manager at the time had this to say after signing the shooting guard: "He's already one of the most recognizable sports figures because of his game, his look, his hunger to win and his style on and off the court." You may have noticed that the adidas executive identified both his "look" and "style" as reasons for the multimillion-dollar deal—two key visual identity pillars.

Around that same time, to promote their *NBA 2K15* game, 2K Sports featured Harden in a television commercial focused entirely on the grooming of his iconic beard. With over 500,000 views on the ad and $200 million in his bank account, Harden would be smart to keep his beard, as it has no doubt contributed to his popularity and success.

who wore it different?

Sometimes simply wearing your uniform in a unique way can become a brand identifier, as was the case for Hall of Fame baseball player Ken Griffey, Jr. Early in his career, Griffey would consistently wear his hat backward during batting practice, a style that divided many baseball fans. The purists resisted, while the younger generation of fans celebrated the rebellious fashion statement. As Griffey approached his Hall of Fame induction, many urged Major League Baseball to feature the former Mariners outfielder in a backward cap on his induction plaque. The request was denied by the league, but that didn't stop "Junior" from putting on a backward hat one last time to conclude his enshrinement speech.

· · ·

Whether it's White embracing his bright-red hair, Harden letting his beard grow, or Griffey turning his hat around, athletes can use their physical appearances to create differentiated brand identities and drive conversation. It's those physical characteristics that we remember the most.

➡ **Accentuate a unique physical feature you were born with like Shaun White.**
➡ **Grow or create your own physical differentiator like James Harden.**
➡ **Wear your uniform in a unique way like Ken Griffey, Jr.**

Ask yourself:

➡ **Do I possess natural physical features that separate me from the rest?**
➡ **Can I adjust my physical features in a way that differentiates me?**
➡ **How can I alter my uniform to create a unique brand identity?**

color coding

Do you have a favorite color? Good. Wear it. Cover your car in it. Paint your house with it. Completely own it. Color is a classic visual identifier used by brands in every industry, but it's exceedingly underutilized by individuals, making it an opportunity for you.

What color do you associate Coca-Cola with? Red? That's not an accident. What color comes to mind when you think of UPS? Brown? Yeah, they did that on purpose too. What about the University of North Carolina? "Carolina Blue," of course. All part of the plan. Your brand should be managed no differently than the way these entities manage themselves. Everything related to these brands is intentional, right down to the deliberate use of a single color. For good reason—according to *Entrepreneur* magazine, "Colors influence how consumers view the 'personality' of the brand in question."

80%

according to a study by Loyola University Maryland, "color increases brand recognition by over 80%."

While color is not often leveraged by individual brands, a select group of icons in both sports and entertainment successfully gained notoriety by consistently wearing a particular color, namely Prince, Johnny Cash, and Tiger Woods.

Prince *was* the color purple

They called Prince "The Purple One" thanks to his hit song "Purple Rain," his feature film of the same name, and not least for his frequent purple-themed fashion statements. The artist, who was known for a time only by a symbol, also became synonymous with a color. When the legendary musician passed away unexpectedly in 2016, "Purple Rain" shot back up to number one on the iTunes download charts more than thirty years after the

athletes are brands too

song's initial release, and the world found itself draped in purple as a tribute to the pop star. From the Staples Center in Los Angeles to the Arts Centre in Melbourne, Australia, buildings and monuments were covered in purple light projections to honor the acclaimed performer.

Not a fluke or an accident. Prince knew what he was doing. By incorporating a single color into all parts of his work and his life, Prince built association with a color to a level rarely seen by personal brands. By doing so, he further differentiated himself from his competition.

Johnny Cash wore black for a reason

Johnny Cash, one of the most renowned country musicians of all time, was known affectionately as "The Man in Black." The phrase came from a song he wrote of the same title and was fueled by his choosing to wear all black on stage and in public. Black became part of Cash's visual identity because he consciously built it into his brand through both his wardrobe and his art.

But black was not chosen without reason. Cash wrote his color-coded song to bring attention to a cause that was near and dear to his heart. His choosing to wear black was meant to be a symbol of rebellion against what he called the "stagnant status quo." The depth of the story surrounding his color choice meant that every time an informed member of the audience saw him in his black garb, they were reminded of his rebellious stance, which ultimately fed back into and built his personal brand story. One may choose a color based simply on preference, but the most strategic brands choose colors that have meaning to who they are and what they stand for.

Tiger Woods owned red on Sunday

Perhaps the most recognizable golfer of all time, Tiger Woods has a few distinct brand identifiers, starting with his first name. But it's a superstition that built another of Woods's most well-known brand symbols: the color red. Woods began wearing red on the final day of his tournaments well before he turned pro, and thanks to years of success, especially in major tournaments like The Masters, Woods was often seen wearing his signature red polo as he putted his way to victory. After years of sporting the color in tournament after tournament and interview after interview, Woods became synonymous with the color red.

Perhaps the most interesting element of this brand identifier comes in its connection to a specific day. Not only does Woods own the color red in his sport, but he's also tied it directly to Sunday, the day when the final round of golf's major tournaments take place. By identifying a specific day in which to reintroduce his signature color, Woods's audience has come to expect and look for the brand mark. Woods has created what we in brand marketing call "episodic content," meaning an idea or story released consistently on a specific day over a period of time. Much like the way we are trained to tune in at the same time on the same day once a week to watch the next episode of our favorite television show, during every major tournament over the course of his career, fans and media expected to see Woods's signature red shining bright on Sundays.

What the colors you wear can say about your personality and brand:

THE COLORS YOU WEAR

BLACK	powerful, sophisticated, a leader and an authority
BLUE	honest, trustworthy, loyal, and smart
BROWN	neutral, stable, steady, and rational
GRAY	reliable, organized, and elegant
RED	passionate, confident, strong-willed, and bold
ORANGE	playful, creative, energetic, and friendly
YELLOW	optimistic, positive, and fun
GREEN	caring, comforting, and generous

• • •

By consistently donning and incorporating a single color into their brand communication strategies, each one of these icons created an additional layer of brand identity and differentiation not found among their competition. Reliability is a critical element of idea retention. Imagine if the corporate executives in Atlanta, Georgia, decided to change the color and design of the Coca-Cola can every day. That daily alteration would cause widespread confusion and make it much harder for consumers to find and identify their favorite soft drink. Constant change does not allow for familiarity and recall.

So why is it that we find it necessary to change our outfits every day, each time making it more difficult for people to identify us? If Coca-Cola were a person, he or she would always wear red. Conversely, if Prince were a soft drink, the bottle would be purple. When it comes to marketing, there is very little difference in how a human or consumer product should be treated. Your brand is no different than the Coke brand. Find a color that best represents who you are and stick to it.

➡ **Pick a color and incorporate it into every part of your life and art like Prince.**
➡ **Give your color a backstory and meaning like Johnny Cash.**
➡ **Assign your color to a specific day like Tiger Woods.**

Ask yourself:

➡ **What's my favorite color?**
➡ **What color best represents the brand I want to portray?**
➡ **Can I give meaning to the color I chose?**

what should I call you?

We may not be able to see a nickname with our eyes, but the labels we use to identify people often create visuals in our minds that either help or hurt a brand. If your nickname is "Super Brat"—as was the case for all-time tennis great John McEnroe—people are going to assume you're tough to deal with whether they know you or not. Your nickname—and the reputation that accompanies it—precedes you. For better or worse, a nickname can stick with you for the rest of your life and become a perception driver for those around you. Because of that, it's important to position your brand in a way that lends itself to an appropriate and beneficial tag. Through consistent behavior and messaging that aligns with your positioning statement, you have a much better chance of garnering a nickname that supports the brand you want to represent.

create your own

When you're Kobe Bryant, coming up with your own nickname doesn't sound that crazy. That's exactly what the legendary former Los Angeles Laker did early on in his career. As a reflection of the turbulence that surrounded his life at the time, Bryant fashioned the "Black Mamba" nickname that is now synonymous with the eighteen-time all-star. So much so that April 13, 2016 (the day Bryant's Lakers hosted the Utah Jazz in his final game) was declared and celebrated as "Mamba Day" by basketball fans and media across the world. Pick your own nickname, get your own day. Not a bad deal and not a bad strategy. If you can pull it off, creating your own nickname like Bryant was able to do can be the most efficient path to a successful moniker.

The question becomes whether "Black Mamba" has relevance off the court now that Bryant is retired. If it doesn't, the equity built into that particular nickname—and along with it part of the Bryant brand—weakens the further he is removed from his playing career. Successful nicknames are those that add to your story regardless of whether you're playing sports or not. When choosing a nickname, choose the one that represents you in all walks of life, not just sports.

a way of life

Former San Antonio Spurs center David Robinson earned a nickname that contributed favorably to his brand on and off the court. Having been a lieutenant, junior grade in the navy prior to his induction into the Naismith Memorial Basketball Hall of Fame, Robinson was christened "The Admiral" during his playing days at the US Naval Academy. The name stuck as he entered the NBA thanks to the exemplary character he would demonstrate in all walks of life.

"The Admiral" would prove to be the perfect representation of Robinson the person while seamlessly illustrating how a nickname can extend a brand beyond athletics. The idea of an admiral in the navy brings with it inherent and exemplary characteristics that no doubt benefited Robinson's reputation. Military officers are presumed to possess higher class, confidence, resilience, intelligence, and grace—the kind of features any sponsor would welcome in a partner. Those characteristics no doubt helped Robinson land endorsement deals with multiple companies over the course of his career, including Nike and Kellogg's. But perhaps more impressive and equally telling is the fact that in 2016, more than ten years after Robinson's retirement from the NBA, another sponsor, Priceline.com, cast him to play a featured role in a commercial to promote its online travel service. Thanks to his consistent storytelling, The Admiral is an example of a personal brand that has remained relevant well after retirement from professional sports.

fit for a king

When used appropriately, nicknames can become powerful mechanisms to enhance the brands they describe. A strategically constructed label should

- ➡ **positively influence your reputation and personal brand,**
- ➡ **elevate your brand to levels those around you aspire to reach, and**
- ➡ **encourage media and fans to follow your every move.**

Thus was born "King James," perhaps the most ambitious nickname of them all. If you're going to call yourself the king, you better be able to back it up, and he has. LeBron James has more than lived up to his royal moniker, having won multiple NBA championships, league MVP awards, and NBA Finals MVP awards. Consistency, frequency, and exceptional performance have paid off for James and his nickname, as "King James" is now a common reference among major sports media outlets. Despite some of the heat journalism has taken over the years, we tend to believe what our favorite news outlets tell us. The more often we see the words *King* and *James* together in headlines, the more likely we are to see LeBron as one of the greatest, if not the greatest, basketball players of all time.

WHEN THE PERFORMANCE MATCHES THE NICKNAME:

"Remembering **KING** James, before and after His Crowning"
—*New York Times*

"The Complete History of Nike LeBron Sneakers Worn by **KING** James"
—Complex

"LeBron Is Truly '**KING** James' When It Comes to NBA Finals Ratings"
—CNN

"See **KING** James' Newest Shoe: The Nike LeBron 13"
—*Sporting News*

"LeBron James Gives a **KING**'s Share of Signature Shoes to Ohio State Football"
—CBS Sports

Note: Emphasis mine.

. . .

Your nickname should be relevant in both sports and in life; a label specific to the game you play does you no good once you retire from that activity. Additionally, when fashioning your own nickname, ensure that the name is a direct reflection of how you intend to position and represent your brand, and live up to that designation twenty-four hours a day. Finally, pick a nickname that will contribute to the sentiment and reputation of your brand. Use it to paint a picture of greatness in the minds of your audience.

➡ **Pick your own nickname and write your own story like Kobe Bryant.**
➡ **Ensure your nickname is authentic and live up to it like David Robinson.**
➡ **Embrace the nickname that takes your brand to new levels like LeBron James.**

Ask yourself:

➡ **Do I currently have a nickname? Does it align with my brand?**
➡ **If I were to choose a nickname, what would it be? Why?**
➡ **When people hear my given or chosen nickname, what do they think?**

what kind of car do you drive?

Brand perception draws from a variety of sources, including the car you drive. According to Complex, vehicle choice says a lot about you: "One way or another, the set of wheels you own represents the type of person you are and the type of life you lead." That preconceived notion could play into your favor as car choice becomes another visual platform from which you can build your brand. According to *Men's Health*, people shop for cars that fit three dimensions of one's self-concept: "who you think you are, who you want to be, and how you'd like others to see you." Those are also the three dimensions critical to a personal brand.

because he's fast

In 2015 world-class sprinter Usain Bolt took to Instagram to show off his newest ride—a 2015 Nissan GT-R, a car that can reach 0–60 mph in less than three seconds. That seems fitting for someone believed to be the fastest man in the world. Bolt suggested as much, writing "Fast knows Fast" in his post. With a name like Bolt, a résumé chock-full of world sprinting records, and countless gold medals, it only makes sense for the legendary speedster to drive one of the fastest cars on the market.

because he's a star

One of the most exciting football players of the last thirty years, Deion Sanders was known simply as "Primetime," a nickname born from his ability to captivate audiences on and off the field, twenty-four hours a day. From his fashion sense to his dance moves, Sanders was all about the glitz and glamour. He once declared a limo as his appropriate mode of transportation, saying, "Sure, we're in limos. We're stars. How else is a star supposed to travel?" As it relates to his flamboyant brand, the answer is absolutely inside of a limo.

because he cares

Leonardo DiCaprio is thought to be worth well over $200 million, yet the Oscar winner can often be seen driving around in a $30,000 Toyota Prius. Why? Because DiCaprio is an avid environmental activist who starred in the 2016 documentary *Before the Flood*, an investigation into the effects of global warming. To drive anything other than an ecologically friendly automobile would be inauthentic to his brand and would counter any of the altruistic work he has done. DiCaprio chose the car that fit his brand, his cause, and his message.

· · ·

Whether it's fast, flashy, or environmentally friendly, the car should match the brand. Before you decide on your automobile of choice, do your research. What are your competitors driving? How can you differentiate yourself while staying authentic to the brand you're trying to build? What reputation does the car you are considering buying bring with it? Remember that with fame comes attention and eyes and cameras, all of which will be pointed at you at all points of the day, including while you're behind the wheel. It's your job to ensure that the attention you garner contributes to the story you're trying to build rather than detracting from it.

➡ **Reinforce your core competency through the car you drive like Usain Bolt.**
➡ **Stay on-brand between the field and the street like Deion Sanders.**
➡ **Stay on message twenty-four hours a day like Leonardo DiCaprio.**

Ask yourself:

➡ **What does my current car say about me? Does it have a reputation?**
➡ **What car would most align with my brand? Why?**
➡ **Does the color of my car match my brand color?**

dress the part

One of the more popular clichés in business is the idea that you should dress for the job you want, not the job you have. Many years ago, when I was a junior marketing executive in San Francisco, my mentor dropped that knowledge on me within weeks after I took my first corporate job. It stuck. From that day forward, I made a point to use my wardrobe to differentiate myself from those around me, always dressing at a level I felt was nicer than the standard surrounding me.

The same philosophy holds true for athletes. Personal presentation can contribute to or take away from your brand perception. *GQ* summed up this idea nicely: "Not only is your confidence [affected] by your clothes, but people make snap judgments about your abilities based on what you're wearing." Use that knowledge to your advantage the next time you dress for a road trip or a night out.

> **❝ People make snap judgments about your abilities based on what you're wearing. ❞** *GQ*

play with perceptions

One of my favorite stunts epitomizes the power of visual storytelling. In a Washington, DC, Metro station in 2007, Joshua Bell, one of the most celebrated violinists in the world at the time, dressed as a "commoner" in street clothes while playing music from the likes of Johann Sebastian Bach. Under normal performance circumstances, Bell would be playing in front of a packed symphony hall, thanks to his stellar talent. However, on this day, over one thousand people would pass by, and not once was there a crowd to bear witness to his greatness. A free show from one of the world's best, yet few would even pause to listen. Why? In simple terms, it was because he didn't look the part.

We tend to fall victim to assumptions and let them cloud our judgment. In this case, why would anyone expect the music in the same metro station they pass through every day on their way to work to be that of a world-renowned artist? Especially one dressed in jeans, a long-sleeved t-shirt, and a baseball cap. People refused to believe that story.

Very few of us would have stopped. Few actually did. In Bell's words: "It was a strange feeling, that people were actually, ah...*ignoring* me." According to Gene Weingarten of the *Washington Post*, who reported on this event back in 2007, Bell's talent could command up to $1,000 a minute. On this day, he would make less than $33 for just short of an hour's work. Not a bad wage for many of us, but nothing compared to his usual haul.

This experiment proves that perception can harm as much as it can help. How well you tell your story will determine how badly people want your product—you.

be bold

It's not often that *GQ* magazine interviews a sideline reporter, but that was the case for the beloved Craig Sager, who was known as much for his fashion sense as his high character and class. Sager, if you're not familiar, was the NBA on TNT reporter who consistently wore the loudest, most colorful suits while interviewing players and coaches. Sager's attire was often so disruptive to the eye that at one point the league actually made him change out of one of his custom-tailored ensembles.

But that's exactly how the strongest and most sustainable brands are built—by creating conversation, standing out from the crowd, and not being afraid to rub some people the wrong way. Sager was comfortable in his own skin, and it showed. A fan and player favorite, the now-passed reporter will always be remembered for his charisma, his passion, and most especially, his suits.

find your moments

One thing that Craig Sager and Russell Westbrook have in common is their flair for the fashionably dramatic. While Sager used his on-air broadcast opportunities as a platform to showcase his style, Westbrook has done an incredible job leveraging pre- and postgame screen time to bring attention to his own eclectic wardrobe. In a sport where there are few on-court opportunities to visually stand out from teammates and competition, Westbrook has found alternate windows to use his employer's popularity to create conversation.

During nearly every nationally televised NBA game in which Westbrook takes part, the camera is sure to capture him and his teammates walking through the tunnel before the contest. The tunnel has become the NBA's version of the red carpet—opportunity. After every game in which Westbrook takes part, there is a press conference attended by every key media outlet, all of which have their cameras rolling—opportunity. As with his shots on the court, Westbrook rarely misses a chance to showcase his now-famous fashion sense off the court. That's especially true in those moments where he finds himself in front of the people who hold the key to his brand's awareness—journalists.

• • •

Joshua Bell teaches us that even the most talented violinist in the world can be disregarded because of how one dresses. Craig Sager teaches us that combining attention-grabbing fashion with professionalism and a rolling camera can forever embed a public figure into the fabric of a sport's culture. Russell Westbrook teaches us that despite the homogeny of team uniforms, there are always windows through which an athlete can showcase one's style and personality.

➡ **Recognize the power of perception like Joshua Bell.**
➡ **Dress loud and proud like Craig Sager.**
➡ **Find the windows for individuality like Russell Westbrook.**

Ask yourself:

➡ **What does my current wardrobe say about me?**
➡ **Does my style match my brand? What improvement can I make?**
➡ **Where will people see my style most often?**

tell me something good

Quotes and phrases have become big business for professional athletes. From New Orleans Pelicans forward Anthony Davis's "Fear the Brow" trademark to Robert Griffin III's ownership of "Unbelievably Believable," athletes have become savvier about their own intellectual property. As ESPN.com describes it, these sayings contribute to the athlete's identity: "It's part of an athlete's brand. It's a business opportunity." Translation: a personal brand mantra can put more money in your pocket.

> **❝ Pro-athletes seek trademarks to make money outside of their careers. ❞** CNN

ride the wave

By the end of his fourth season, Kirk Cousins had thrown for a mere 7,196 yards and forty-seven touchdowns. Dan Marino, Peyton Manning, and Tom Brady had all thrown for more touchdowns than that in a single season. That's not to say that Kirk Cousins is not a great quarterback; he may

athletes are brands too

ultimately go down as one of the greatest passers of his generation. Time will tell. However, the amazing thing about his career and brand is that I can say or type the words "You like that!" and a number of you reading this book will recognize that as a quote from Cousins himself, one he uttered following a 2015 victory in which he helped rally his Washington teammates back from a 24–0 deficit against the Tampa Bay Buccaneers. Because of the popularity of the video featuring Cousins hollering the now-famous phrase, the quarterback will likely always be known as much for his mouth as his arm. Thank you, social media.

What you say matters. And yes, once the phrase caught on with fans and the media alike, Cousins did indeed file for a trademark. According to Fox Sports, it covers the phrase for use on billboards, bumper stickers, decals and stickers for home decor, magnetic bumper stickers, posters, t-shirts, and hooded sweatshirts. Get yours, Kirk.

speak your own language

In what has to be one of the all-time greatest responses to a postgame interview question, Bryce Harper once uttered these immortal words: "That's a clown question, bro." If I could insert the laughing hysterically emoji here without losing credibility and your trust, I would. Though I do not believe the question matters, given the gold that was the response, I will share it. After Harper hit a home run in the game prior, a Canadian reporter asked the (at the time) nineteen-year-old if he would be enjoying a "celebratory Canadian beer." Doesn't sound like it.

The Washington Nationals PR department may have cringed once those words left their young star's lips, but I say embrace it. Harper appears to be one of the most authentic athletes in sports, polarizing as he may be. He's an individual who does not often mince words, and despite some who might dislike him for it, as a brand marketer, I applaud him.

You know who else applauds him for his candid remarks? Teenage baseball players. Harper burst onto the Major League Baseball scene as a teenager himself, and it's that generational authenticity combined with his

MVP-level performance and exposure that creates a differentiated position. How many times have we heard the notion that baseball is boring? Old? Stodgy? The game has lacked a youthful voice for years, which makes this the perfect era for an athlete like Harper to speak his mind. And while he's speaking his mind, he's building his brand—love it or hate it.

yes, we can make America great again

In a country nearly split down the middle, it can be hard to find commonalities between the two main political parties in the United States. That's why you might have a difficult time believing me when I say that I see similarities between presidents Barack Obama and Donald Trump. You think I've lost my mind, right? Maybe. But think about it—what did each president use to help win the presidency?

Marketing.

It's just that most of us didn't realize it, which happens to be the calling card of a great marketer. It would be naïve for us to think that marketing does not have a hand in the determination of a country's president-elect. There's a reason we call the platforms they run on presidential "campaigns," which is the same word marketers use to describe advertising. That commercial you saw earlier today? That's a television campaign. That ad you saw in that magazine? That's a print campaign. That thirty-second radio spot you heard on the way to work? Yep, that's a radio campaign.

You know what else is a campaign? Obama's "Yes We Can." As was Trump's "Make America Great Again." Those are nothing more than taglines, and neither had anything to do with policy. But policies are boring, hard to understand, and quite honestly just too political for most people. Few of us work as politicians. Only a fraction of our population majored in political science and even fewer have experience in foreign relations. But the majority of us are experienced in consuming advertising. We eat it up.

Taglines take complicated ideas and make them easy to understand and retain. "Yes We Can" was a derivative of "Hope"—another of Obama's famous taglines during his time running for office. Guess what concept

"Make America Great Again" derives from? Hope. When you break it down to their core messages, both Barack Obama and Donald Trump ran on similar platforms. They each promised hope, something the average person can understand and get behind.

. . .

These are all examples of the impact one phrase can have on an individual's brand. Sayings, expressions, and quotes are no different than taglines as they relate to a company or product. Athlete brands can and should have taglines. Just as Apple says "Think Different" and Verizon once asked its audience "Can You Hear Me Now?" athletes deserve a phrase that speaks to who they are and what makes them unique. When Apple urges you to think different, they are doing so based on the fact that they are consistently bringing fresh and new thinking to an industry that can sometimes feel commoditized. Verizon asked "Can You Hear Me Now?" to bring attention to their superior coverage across the United States. Neither of these mega-brands are saying things for the sake of saying them; they are pronouncing what makes them unique among their competition. By doing so, they're bringing in new fans, customers, and ambassadors.

Athletes are brands, and brands need succinct messaging to declare what makes them unique and desirable to a community. People like to say, "Keep it simple, stupid"; I prefer "Keep it stupid simple." Your tagline needs to be understood with little to no effort. The moment I have to think about what you're trying to tell... Well, I already lost interest. We live in a world where humans have shorter attention spans than goldfish (yes, that's true). I don't want to hear your life story, and I don't want to hear sixty minutes of political jargon. Society is driven by sound bites, so give us something we can sink our teeth into quickly or you risk being ignored.

- ➡ When you say something that catches on, capitalize on it like Kirk Cousins.
- ➡ Embrace who you are and put it into words like Bryce Harper.
- ➡ Keep your message simple, clear, and relatable like Barack Obama and Donald Trump.

Ask yourself:

- ➡ Am I currently known for a saying or phrase? Do I have a favorite?
- ➡ Do I have a unique voice or way of speaking? If so, how is it unique?
- ➡ Is my phrase clear? Is my voice relatable to a significant population?

raise your hand

When a person positions their fingers into the shape of horns, as sports fans our minds instantly go to the Texas Longhorns. When someone connects their hands at the thumbs in the shape of the letter *U*, the Miami Hurricanes come to mind. And when an individual throws up the letter *V* using their index and middle fingers, we as sports fans don't always assume it to be a peace sign; rather, it's a *V* for victory to represent the University of Southern California.

Hand gestures can be powerful brand tools, especially in the sports world. Not only are they effective at identifying allegiance, but they also do a tremendous job of connecting people from all walks of life and all parts of the world. We as humans want to be part of something greater than ourselves, which is why sports are such a major part of our society. Like the aforementioned schools, develop a hand gesture of your own that rallies your community around you and your brand.

your bat signal

While the director of brand marketing for adidas football and baseball, I set out to tap into the need for identification and to establish a visual representation of the love athletes had for our brand. Having seen several employees put up three fingers (representing the brand's iconic three stripes) to show their affiliation with the company by way of social media, it occurred to me that a simple hand gesture like this could connect the brand's most passionate fans while demonstrating to those yet to pledge their allegiance to the company just how strong the adidas family was.

Five years after putting that idea into a presentation, and through countless football camps and athlete photo shoots where we featured the three-finger visual in as many pieces of content as possible, it became organic. Five years later, high school and college athletes were voluntarily throwing up three fingers in front of the camera. At the same time, our professional athlete partners were posting pictures of themselves with three fingers waving proudly in the air, tagging their photos with another sign of allegiance we ignited in football: "#teamadidas."

The three-finger hand gesture became our brand's bat signal.

Though sizeable entities like universities and corporations most often use this approach, it can and should also be leveraged by individual athletes. Kids want to emulate their favorite players while they play the sports they love. By giving your fans a gesture to represent you while connecting the community that follows you, you're garnering free exposure in basketball gyms, hockey rinks, and swimming pools all over the country and in some cases the world. Once you've identified what it is you want to rally your community around, find a way to make it visual with your hands.

with feeling

Much like the three fingers that represent adidas's three stripes, John Cena of the WWE uses a three-finger hand gesture to represent the tenets he believes to be authentic to his own brand: hustle, loyalty, and respect. The

Cena hand signal is a great example of using a gesture to bring attention and contribute to a personal brand story. Rather than simply forming the letter *C* with his hand to denote the first letter of his last name, Cena instead crafted something deeper and more meaningful to his story. Better still, the "hustle, loyalty, respect" that the three fingers symbolize also happen to align with his most famous catchphrase, giving Cena a seamless "see (his hands) and say (his words)" brand story.

own it. literally.

Gareth Bale is one of the highest-paid soccer players in the world, but it's not just his feet that are paying the bills. Ironically, Bale's hands have been projected to contribute some £3 million a year to his bank account. Bale has become known for his characteristic goal celebration, in which the Wales national team forward makes a heart shape with his hands, a gesture honoring his childhood sweetheart. It's a celebration and symbol that has become iconic for Bale, so much so that, like Kirk Cousins, he applied to trademark the gesture for use on clothing, jewelry, and headgear. It was a strategic personal branding move that could keep him financially secure for years beyond his athletic career.

· · ·

These examples and teachings are not and should not be mutually exclusive. Your goal in developing your own gesture is to create a symbol that accomplishes and combines these three lessons. First, create a symbol that encourages and breeds community rather than simply developing another mechanism for personal identification. Second, use your gesture to tell a story that is in line with the brand you are trying to build and one that creates an emotional bond among those within your newfound community. Finally, trademark it. If you are successful in creating a passionate community rallied around a cause or an idea, others will no doubt try to replicate your concept and benefit from it financially. Protect yourself, protect your work, and protect your message.

- ➡ **Connect your community through a consistent visual like adidas football.**
- ➡ **Tell a brand story that speaks to who you are like John Cena.**
- ➡ **Trademark your symbol and protect its integrity like Gareth Bale.**

Ask yourself:

- ➡ **Do I use hand gestures to communicate? Which do I use the most?**
- ➡ **Is there a hand gesture I can adopt as my own?**
- ➡ **Does my hand gesture have meaning? Is it aligned with my brand?**

adopt an emoji

According to Swyft Media, 6 billion emoticons or stickers (let's call them emojis) are sent around the world every day. I could probably just stop here, point made. Emojis are popular. And Swyft just gave you 6 billion reasons to incorporate them into your social media strategy. But I have another idea. What I propose is not to simply add emojis for the sake of a trend but instead to find an existing emoji that most closely resembles something inherent to your brand and own it. It could be the color you're trying to associate with, it could be a flag that represents your culture, or it could be that slightly creepy man emoji with the mustache that happens to look just like you. Whatever it may be, pick one and seize control of it.

92%

according to a report by Emogi, "92% of online consumers use emoji."

How can you own an emoji? By consistent and frequent usage, of course! (My two friends consistency and frequency are never too far away.) By now, every prominent athlete has a Twitter, Instagram, or Snapchat account. Each platform brings with it a canvas on which emojis can be painted. If you're one of the fortunate individuals with an obvious emoji connection, start now. Every post from this day forward should incorporate that emoji in one way or another, whether it is a sign-off for a social post or integrated into the body of your message. After a while, I guarantee, your fans will begin to see that visual as an extension of your brand and start using it to identify you through their own social channels.

In 2016, ESPN reporter Darren Rovell had some fun by teaming up with creative agency Laundry Service to develop what *Sporting News* described as "the ultimate player emoji chart" focused entirely on assigning emojis to current and former NBA players. While it may have been meant to be a joke, some of the suggested pairings represent legitimate opportunities for athletes to own an emoji. A favorite of mine is Dwyane Wade, also known as "The Flash," who in this chart is represented by the lightning bolt symbol that also famously symbolizes the DC Comics character of the same name. It would not take much time for fans of Wade to start using the mark to represent the former Miami Heat star, assuming he also used it himself.

• • •

According to a report by Emogi, 92 percent of the online population uses emoji as a form of communication. As incredible as it may seem, emojis are

athletes are brands too

now part of our global language, which makes it imperative for you as an aspiring brand to use this messaging phenomenon to your advantage.

➡ **Choose an emoji that best visualizes your brand position.**
➡ **Incorporate your emoji into every social media post across all platforms.**
➡ **Pick an emoji that represents you in sport *and* in life, not one or the other.**

Ask yourself:

➡ **Which emoji best visualizes my brand position?**
➡ **Does my chosen emoji have an existing reputation? Is it on-brand?**
➡ **Does my chosen emoji represent me in *and* out of sports?**

get verified

We love to judge a book by its cover. And by book, I mean people. And by cover, I mean anything superficial, including whether you're verified on Twitter, Instagram, or any other social media platform. Yes, I'm serious. That little blue check mark has become one of the most sought-after pieces of digital currency in today's social media–driven world. Like I said, perception is reality, and the reality is if you don't have that particular shade of blue next to your name, people take you less seriously.

1%

as of July 2016, less than 1% of Twitter users were verified.

Marketing is a perception game. The better you are at playing the game, the more doors will open for you. Get out there and apply for your authentication while you're relevant. Your role in athletics makes you a prime candidate on a platform like Twitter, which describes its blue check mark as an identifier that "lets people know that an account of public interest is authentic." One of the industries included in the "key interest areas" in which the company chooses to verify individuals happens to be sports.

Your perception is your reality.

With less than 1 percent of the total Twitter user base having that blue check next to their name, the numbers prove that verification remains a symbol of social influence. Once again, athletics has provided you with an opportunity to differentiate yourself from the crowd. And once again, your time to take advantage of that influence is now.

athletes are brands too

objective #2:
create the most
conversation

The key to brand awareness in today's social media–driven world is conversation, which also happens to be our second objective. If people are talking about you, you're relevant. If they're not, you're not.

With that in mind, the one objective I've included in just about every marketing plan I've led is to be the most talked-about brand within a certain frame of reference and during a given window of time. For example, one objective for a graduating college football athlete heading into the off-season may be to become the most talked-about wide receiver (frame of reference) during the NFL Scouting Combine (window of time). If at the end of the event he ends up being the most talked-about player at his position, then he no doubt has an edge on the competition. General managers, coaches, and the media will all have his name on the brain, which is an enviable position to be in for anyone entering the NFL Draft. At the very least, conversation gives you a chance. If people aren't thinking about you, you might as well not exist. If you're an athlete

If people are talking about you, you're relevant. If they're not, you're not.

competing with a number of other athletes for the spotlight, I would suggest making conversation a part of your objective set going into every year.

I've broken down some of the strategies and tactics I have used in the past to ensure my brands dominate the social media and journalistic airwaves.

family first

Your first task is to build a community—the people who follow you, root for you, and endorse you every step of the way. As a brand, these are the people who make up your extended family. Without them, you don't exist.

A common mistake of many newly minted brands and companies is to skip the community-building step and jump straight into advertising. Too often brands will forget to earn people's trust and bond, instead opting to make an attempt at paying for that love via advertising. The problem is that it takes a tremendous amount of money and consistent messaging to establish a brand in this way. Most of us won't pay much attention to an ad or even remember the ad until we've seen it multiple times. That can be the case for television, print, or any other form of promotion. Few newborn companies, and even fewer personal brands, can begin with an advertising-led strategy and survive the financial burden that comes with it.

On the rare occasion that a company or individual does have enough money to survive the cost of a long-term campaign, it's unlikely that the message will resonate without peer-to-peer recommendations, which happen to be the most trusted form of advertising still today. We listen to our friends more than we listen to brands or the people selling us on something. As a result, for a campaign to truly connect with a consumer group, there needs to be a foundation of ambassadors ready to support the brand's message and sing its praises.

Take a look at the following hypothetical conversations between John and his good friend Jane, and ask yourself which of these two scenarios is more likely to lead to a purchase by John.

> **JOHN:** Have you seen those commercials for that new sports drink?
>
> **JANE:** Yeah, I've seen them! I don't know what it is, though.

Or

> **JOHN:** Have you seen those commercials for that new sports drink?
>
> **JANE:** Yeah, I've seen them! I've actually been drinking it for a while now and *love* it.

3 billion
according to Jonah Berger in his book *Contagious*, Americans "mention specific brands more than 3 billion times a day."

John is of course going to be more likely to try the new drink if it comes with the endorsement of his close companion. If you want someone's allegiance, gain the support of his or her friends and build a surrounding community of passionate and vocal followers. Those are the individuals who will sing your praises and support your point of view on the subjects you truly believe in. Passion produces passion, which means the more avid people are about you and your personal brand, the more likely that community of adoring followers is to grow organically. With that growth comes a louder voice for you in the marketplace.

Build your community of followers before you build a print ad.

your tribe called...

If you're going to position yourself as an influencer, you need to look the part, including how you appear in your social media profiles. In today's digital world, size indeed matters. The bigger your following is, the bigger your reputation is and the stronger your perception is. This is the tribe that will carry your reputation, even if things get ugly. And while it may sound daunting, building an impressive following of your own is a much easier process than it may seem. Start with these methods I've used myself over the years.

identify your target market.

Identify and target those communities within which you hold influence. Begin by revisiting the pyramids of influence, which I introduced in chapter 1 and bring back again here. Everyone south of your point on the pyramids encompasses your potential ambassador community; these segments of the population make up your target market.

Athletes beneath your placement on the below pyramid of influence make up your pool of athletes to target. (Mark where you sit on this chart, and draw an arrow from that point down.)

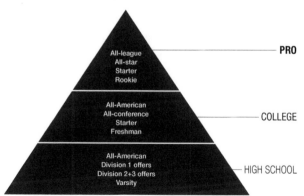

POTENTIAL **ATHLETE** AMBASSADORS

All-league
All-star
Starter
Rookie
— **PRO**

All-American
All-conference
Starter
Freshman
— COLLEGE

All-American
Division 1 offers
Division 2+3 offers
Varsity
— HIGH SCHOOL

athletes are brands too

Fans beneath your placement on the below pyramid of influence make up your pool of fans to target. (Mark where you sit on this chart, and draw an arrow from that point down.)

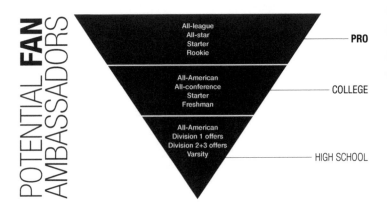

"like" their content

Once you've identified your target audience, start interacting with them through your preferred (and brand-appropriate) social channels. By showing love to the individuals within these groups, your chances of gaining followers increase. You don't have to play the "follow back" game (although you can) to drive up your numbers; instead, simply "like" the agreeable content being pushed out by the people you're looking to win over. A "like" is essentially an invisible action on most platforms, but it serves as a notification to the person you are supporting. That does two things: first, it brings you to their attention; and second, by showing them love, it incentivizes them to follow you.

keep engaging

Once you do create a following, people are more likely to interact with you, and that's a good thing. Nurture your newfound relationships. The more you show love to your fans and followers, the more likely they are to support and share your content while often publicly singing your praises—all because you pushed the "like" button on one of their posts. That public endorsement will encourage those within their network to follow you as well. Your duty to engage with your fans doesn't stop once they follow you.

A strong social community will put you in an enviable position. The more followers you have, the further your voice will reach and the more likely the industries you're trying to break into will take notice. This moves you one step closer to pursuing your passion full-time.

❝ If a tree falls in the forest and no one is there, does it still make a sound? ❞
unknown

allow me to reintroduce myself

With as much inherent influence as athletes have, unfortunately it doesn't completely excuse them from the need to network. If you're the starting outside linebacker for the Miami Dolphins but want to build a personal brand around your love of fishing, your ability to get to the quarterback alone is not going to convince fishing fanatics of your capacity to reel in the next big one. You need to prove your worth, and you need endorsements. That's where networking comes in.

While in the midst of your playing career (starting as early as high school), it becomes crucial for you to network and build relationships within the industry you're looking to crack into. As is the case in any sport, there's an influential 1 percent in every trade. Fortunately, they tend to run in packs. Find out where those key gathering moments are and finagle your way into them. Introduce yourself to as many people as you can.

Your athletic résumé will open doors not available to the average person, but that window of opportunity is once again a small one. If the average NFL career is three years, and assuming our outside linebacker was a four-year starter in college, he is likely looking at about seven years of relevance and true influence. Those seven years become the most significant years for establishing his brand outside of football. Once that window closes, if he hasn't already made inroads in the sport of fishing, he'll be starting from square one. Advantage lost.

As is the case in so many scenarios, it's not what you know, it's who you know. Start now.

earn R.E.S.P.E.C.T.

I started writing my first book because I loved the subject and I was passionate about building athletic brands. However, I also knew that by writing and publishing a book, I would receive a certain level of legitimacy within the industry that I ultimately wanted to become part of. I recognized that, good or bad, having a book often elevated the author in the minds of his or her audience. Perhaps as important, the book opened doors to influencers within the industry who may have otherwise not returned calls. I was suddenly connected to people in and around athletics that I had no relationship to previously.

Your influence within your sport will provide you with just enough intrigue to get your foot in the door, but it's not enough. You need a platform to speak from. You need to prove your worth and authenticity within the community you're looking to join. You need to earn respect. Create your own public voice, and build the reputation of a thought leader.

That doesn't mean you need to write a book, although I would encourage anyone to put his or her passion on paper. In today's digital age, there are endless opportunities to find platforms to speak from that take less time and less investment than a book. Additionally, more and more of the major media outlets are giving athletes a voice to communicate on a variety of subjects.

Derek Jeter, for example, formed The Players' Tribune to "provide athletes with a platform to connect directly with their fans, in their own words." With these outlets come, in many cases, significant audiences, which means you are not responsible for finding readers.

If you are passionate about a subject, then you no doubt have an opinion. That opinion will drive your narrative. Write it down and pitch media outlets that align with your brand and bring with them the appropriate audience.

• • •

Your brand is only as strong and sustainable as your audience is large and adoring. I've always been a proponent of quality over quantity, meaning I will never encourage someone to fabricate a following that is actually not inter- ested in what the athlete has to say. Rather, I steer clients toward attracting the right audience members who will engage and support them. However, the reality is that the bigger that targeted audience is, the more powerful and further-reaching the voice. Time is once again of the essence. While you're resting, someone else is building an army. So get out and start building your community today, before it's too late.

WHICH DO YOU THINK HAS THE **BETTER PIZZA?**

A's PIZZA

B's PIZZA

Your social channel is no different than a packed restaurant. The more people you have following you, the more people will assume you're worth following.

Perception matters.

athletes are brands too

- ➡ **Establish a perception of influence through a strong social media following.**
- ➡ **Build personal relationships with the most influential people in the industry.**
- ➡ **Develop a public voice through an existing outlet or by creating your own.**

Ask yourself:

- ➡ **What does my current following number say about my relevance?**
- ➡ **What influencers do I know within the industry I'm passionate about?**
- ➡ **Where and how can I build authenticity within my industry of passion?**

talk early, often, and always

Every time I set out to be the most talked-about brand within a given moment or period of time, I would support that goal with this strategy: talk early, often, and always. Just as it suggests, there are three parts to the plan.

while you were sleeping

How many times have you seen an NFL replay in which the defensive end or outside linebacker times the snap so perfectly that he's sprinted past the offensive lineman before the poor guy has had a chance to move? The best pass rushers in the league consistently get a jump on their competition. Brands are no different.

Talking early is about creating a conversation with your audience before your competition is ready to react. In my own experience with product launches, our team could often forecast when our rivals were going to begin to heavy up on their messaging. Typically, it's a couple of months prior to when a given target audience is about to make their purchases for the year. For instance, if you're selling football cleats, you know that athletes will start practice in the fall, which means the shopping season begins in the weeks immediately preceding that. Within that shopping window will come a barrage of brands banging down social media doors looking for sales. As a marketer, recognizing that conversation cadence allows me to be strategic in my own timing. That knowledge helps me get a jump on my competition, just like that linebacker.

Athletes can be just as predictable. Typically individuals are going to be more active leading up to, during, and immediately following the season (depending on the outcome). In most sports, that leaves a few months of quiet. What I would suggest to you is to get ahead of your counterparts. While they're reveling in the quiet period, start talking. By doing so you will avoid all of the clutter and noise that surrounds the beginning of a new season and have the audience all to yourself—an audience that is no doubt dying for content from their favorite sport.

often. often. often.

Second comes the need to create a consistent flow of conversation through your channels and with your community. It's not enough to get out of the gates ahead of your competitors; you must get ahead and *stay* ahead by being active throughout the days, weeks, and months. The warning here is not to talk for the sake of talking but to provide your audience with content that adds insight and value to their lives in some way. If cooking is your passion, you have three meals a day to share with your audience. Show them and tell them something they don't know about you or about cooking— that's what they signed up for.

7

one marketing principle called the "Rule of 7" suggests that it takes seven points of contact before someone will buy a product or act on a call to action.

365

Finally, "always on" means creating fresh content every single day of the year. The reality is that building a brand is not easy; if it were, everyone would have a signature shoe. But with a little work on the front end, you'll find yourself miles ahead of your rivals and well on your way to that custom sneaker with your name on the tongue.

Start by building a content calendar for the year (I know, scary—but worth it). On that calendar first determine what your story is going to be at a high level. Next, decide what the content for each of those stories will be (a photo, a video, a piece of art, text only, etc.). Finally, write your copy. Do this for every day of the year. It sounds heavy—and it is—but by doing so, the pressure to come up with something interesting to say each day is lifted. If you already know what you're going to talk about on March 16, you are free from having to rack your brain for what to post on that day. While your competition is scrambling to find something interesting to say, you're simply pushing a button.

Moreover, by being prepared and having content planned well in advance, you are also able to be reactive. When something newsworthy happens in the world or in your life that you want to respond to, you can because you have the time. You're not worried about planning for the next day or the next week. You've already built your plan for the year.

. . .

I can guarantee that there is a substantial portion of your competition that is not putting in this level of work to build their brand. If you adopt the same hardworking attitude that you've embraced for your sport and apply it to your brand, you will win. While the unprepared are struggling to find a place in the world after their careers end, you'll be moving right into your new role as an influencer in an industry you love.

➡ **Talk to your audience before your competition has a chance to react.**
➡ **Give your audience content throughout the day, week, and month.**
➡ **Keep the conversation between you and your audience going 365.**

Ask yourself:

➡ **Am I being strategic with the timing of my social media posts?**
➡ **Am I being consistent with my social media posts?**
➡ **Are each of my social media posts supporting my brand story?**

living social

If you're posting the same content on Twitter as you are on Instagram, Facebook, or any other channel, stop. Immediately. You're setting yourself up for a social media fall from grace. Think about your own experience with the brands or personalities you follow socially. You likely follow at least one of those entities on multiple channels; now what good does it do you as a member of that audience to see the same photos or videos on Twitter *and* Instagram? None. If anything it may annoy you to the point where you might even consider unfollowing the person or brand because of the repetitiveness.

I've always been a champion of diagnosing the inherent advantages of each platform and building content that specifically leverages those benefits. Take Instagram, a space built to showcase beautiful visuals. It's a platform where creative people flourish and flock, which means the audience is going to be looking for and expecting premium photo and video from you. Every piece of content you push out on this particular channel should be driven by a visual, and every visual should be of the highest quality. Ask yourself: Would my audience print this out and put it on their wall? Would they make it their phone background? Does it tell a story consistent with my personal brand? If the answer to any of those questions is no, then reconsider your post or contemplate another social media outlet.

On the flip side, think of Twitter as the social media fusion of CNN and reality TV. It's a place for real-time news while at the same time offering a 140-character glimpse into the inner workings of your favorite celebrity minds. Twitter provides a more shareable experience than a platform like Instagram, which allows for "likes" and comments but does not offer a user the ability to easily distribute their favorite content. Twitter was built on and thrives from a foundation of idea sharing. With that in mind, use Twitter in a different way than you would any other platform. Twitter becomes an effective space for brand announcements. Are you committing to play for a particular university? Use Twitter and watch the news spread. Are you signing a free agent contract with a new team? Use Twitter and watch the news spread. Are you retiring from professional sports altogether? Use Twitter and watch the news spread.

2.95 billion

the projected number of social media users across the globe by 2020, according to Statista

tell me

On February 7, 2016, *Sporting News* asked, "Did Marshawn Lynch just announce his retirement on Twitter?"

Yes. Yes, he did.

A man of few words, Marshawn Lynch took to Twitter to broadcast the (at the time) end of his career by simply posting a "peace sign" emoji and a photo of a pair of football cleats hanging from a telephone wire. I can't imagine a more perfectly designed declaration of retirement for an athlete known for his refusal to answer questions from the media. Would it have been authentic for Lynch to hold a press conference? Not at all. Would it have made sense to write a long-winded social media diatribe reminiscing on his career? Not for an athlete who keeps his private life private. Would it have been genuine for Lynch to suddenly change his laid-back, playful tone and personality? It's just not who he is. Peace sign. Hanging cleats. Goodbye, football. Perfect.

The results reflected the execution as Lynch's tweet generated over 200,000 retweets and over 200,000 likes. Right story, right platform. Compare that to the 21,000 likes Baltimore wide receiver Steve Smith received on an Instagram post hinting to his own retirement. Right story, wrong platform.

athletes are brands too

Match your story and content with the right social media outlet and watch as your news spreads. Pick the wrong space and watch it fade into obscurity.

show me

If you're a photographer, you're on Instagram.

If you're a graphic designer, you're on Instagram.

If you're a sneakerhead, yep, you're on Instagram.

Why? Because Instagram is the most visually driven of all the social platforms. Not to mention that it's huge. As of January 2017, Instagram had amassed 150 million daily active users, making it the perfect platform for someone looking to tell a graphic story. Someone like Joe Haden, NFL cornerback and renowned sneakerhead. It's no coincidence that Haden has more followers on Instagram than he does on Twitter. His off-field brand is very much influenced by his impressive sneaker collection.

Nor is it a surprise that every major sneaker blog has exponentially more followers on Instagram than on Twitter. They thrive off posting photos representing the latest shoe drop. Nor is it a surprise that the most well-known athletic shoe customizers have more followers on Instagram than on Twitter. We want to see their latest works of art. Key word here being *see*.

According to Entrepreneur.com, "Brands increasingly find that their customers crave visual content, as evidenced by the popularity of social platforms such as Instagram." Twitter is about the news; Instagram is about the art.

FOLLOWERS BY **SOCIAL PLATFORM**

	Type	Twitter	Instagram	Change
Joe Haden	Sneakerhead	426,000	624,000	+46%
DJ Clark Kent	Sneakerhead	92,100	152,000	+65%
Sole Collector	Sneaker Blog	478,000	1.6MM	+235%
Nice Kicks	Sneaker Blog	794,000	2.8MM	+253%
Mache Custom Kicks	Customizer	31,900	544,000	+1,605%
Soles by Sir	Customizer	1,853	51,000	+2,652%
Kickasso	Customizer	9,077	550,000	+5,959%

Note: Numbers are accurate as of September 6, 2017.

If you are looking to build your personal brand within a visually driven industry like fashion or photography or graphic design, use the platform that does the best job of presenting your work. Today, that platform is Instagram. Tomorrow it might be something else, and if it changes, so should you.

entertain me

If you want to create influence among a teenage audience (and you should), YouTube might be your best bet. According to a 2014 survey by *Variety*, teenagers found YouTube stars to be more influential than any of the so-called traditional celebrities such as Jennifer Lawrence and Leonardo DiCaprio. In fact, the top-five most influential figures named in the survey were all YouTubers.

The world is changing and, once again, so should you. We often assume that TV dominates our view of the world, and in a lot of ways it can. But the reality is that for the generations following us, digital stars are going to continue to be as relevant as those spawned in Hollywood. Perhaps more. You, as an athlete, will face the same scenario as Lawrence and DiCaprio. How can you maintain—better yet, *grow*—your influence among the generations to come? Build your own content and tell your own stories. That's how.

athletes are brands too

Use YouTube in the same way these digital stars are using the platform. In 2017 Samsung partnered with another YouTube celebrity, Casey Neistat, to produce a commercial that captured the essence of today's homegrown digital producers in one of the more inspiring commercials, for me personally, as a self-proclaimed creator of a different kind. In the commercial, Neistat had this to say: "We know it's not the size of the production that matters, it's what you make."

So many athletes aspire to be on television. So many dream of starring in a big Hollywood production or landing a role on a hit television show. But why? For the celebrity? Many of you already are celebrities. To have a voice? Do you really think your voice will come through authentically after being filtered by the corporate machines pumping out these multimillion-dollar projects? For your brand? The only brand that matters when working for a production giant is the brand at the top of the script. Not yours.

> **The screen that matters fits in your pocket and the director is you.**

If you want to become an on-screen star, do it. In today's world, nothing is stopping you. The only difference is, in today's world, the screen that matters fits in your pocket and the director is you.

• • •

The days of media monopolization are over. No longer are athletes limited to television, radio, and the mere handful of nationally relevant newspapers to build their brand. The idea of pitching a story to one of those publications is gone as well. The truth is the people have taken back control of the world's voice thanks to social media. You control your story line. You can say what you want, when you want, and where you want, and that message can reach millions instantly. The challenge lies in the how. The best way to curate a voice that cuts through the noise is to have a strategy that cuts through the noise. By leveraging each platform differently and uniquely, you give your audience a reason to follow you on each. With that additional connectivity comes further interaction potential between you and the ever-powerful people.

➡ **Use Twitter to announce your biggest moments like Marshawn Lynch.**
➡ **Use Instagram to visualize your passion like Joe Haden.**
➡ **Use YouTube to make your own movies like Casey Neistat.**

Ask yourself:

➡ **How many social media platforms am I on?**
➡ **Which social media platforms best align with my brand? Why?**
➡ **Am I using each platform differently and posting unique content to each?**

spend money to make money

In life you have to take risks in order to reap the biggest rewards. In business you have to spend money to make money. And in brand marketing you have to invest in the brand to build the brand. Whether you make millions playing in the NBA or minimum wage as a part-time student, there are dollars to be allocated to marketing. The question is whether you are being critical with your money as it is currently being spent. For those of you without reporters and fans beating down your door and who haven't yet taken a budget risk or found ways to increase your presence, I ask: Why not? What do you have to lose?

Are you investing in consultation from brand-marketing experts (whether through their written works or on a one-on-one basis), or are you expecting to improve without outside points of view? Are you finding new ways to develop content (whether through investing in the technology to create your own or paying for third-party creative development), or are you expecting your social following to entertain itself?

> ❝ An investment in knowledge pays the best interest. ❞ Benjamin Franklin

I often hear athletes tell me they want to build their brand, yet the changes that they are willing to make are nothing more than safe. Few are willing to invest in marketing in order to help turn things around. If you're not willing to invest in marketing, how do you expect marketing to help you? How do you expect your brand to grow? The old way of thinking no longer works; the competition is just too fierce. If you want to break through the clutter in today's landscape, you're going to have to spend the dollars necessary.

If you want to be influential in your industry of choice, build a stronger brand.

If you want to build a stronger brand, invest in marketing.

along came athlete

Full disclosure: this concept was inspired by the Ben Stiller movie *Along Came Polly*. If you're not familiar, put the book down and watch it as soon as possible. In the movie, Philip Seymour Hoffman plays Sandy Lyle, a former child actor who's trying to resurrect his fleeting career as an adult by hiring his own documentary film crew. Something along the lines of ESPN's *30 for 30* series.

But since I can't even watch a movie (a comedy, no less) without thinking of ways to build brands, Hoffman's character got me thinking. Why couldn't an athlete hire his or her own film crew? More importantly, why *wouldn't* an athlete? The numbers around video consumption on the internet are staggering. According to Cisco, video will account for 80 percent of global internet traffic by 2019. *Huh?* Nearly 1 million minutes will be shared every second. *I'm sorry, what?* It would take an individual 5 million years to watch all the video that will be shared each month. *Come again?* Yeah, the folks at Hootsuite said it best: video *is* the internet.

80%
according to Cisco, video will account for 80% of global internet traffic by 2019.

Those stats would suggest that hiring a personal film crew to create video content is an investment worth making. If video is the future, it in turn becomes a crucial avenue for you to build your brand. Do you want to be known for the work you do in the community? Bring your film crew with you the next time you hand out turkeys on Thanksgiving. Do you want to be known as a sneakerhead? Bring your film crew with you the next time you stop by your local boutique for the latest drop. Do you want to be known as an outdoorsman? Bring your film crew with you the next time you become one with nature. Do that and I promise you this: the next time you tell your story, prospective brands will be watching and imagining a world in which you're endorsing their product in your next video.

content is your king
A social channel without content is like a book with blank pages. Simply having a Twitter or Instagram account isn't enough; it's your job to deliver

your audience a dynamic story through each platform. That's where content comes in: photos, videos, animations, and the more traditional written word. If people are following you, they've opted in, meaning they've publicly declared their desire to hear from you. Talk to them. Talk with them. Have fun.

That's exactly what Chris Bosh did. In 2008, the Toronto Raptors forward was on the brink of making his third All-Star Game. To leave nothing to chance, Bosh took to YouTube to generate fan support and ultimately votes. He created a campaign video in which he impersonated a used-car salesman, urging fans to get out and vote for him. The content did its job, as Bosh was selected to the game, while unknowingly starting a trend. Today it's not uncommon to find similar all-star campaign videos pop up across every major sport.

Be your own publicist. Create your own content. Tell your own stories.

own it

Straight Outta Compton, the 2015 smash hit movie about rap group N.W.A., a unit fronted by Dr. Dre and Ice Cube, earned over $200 million. The film also became (at the time) the highest-grossing movie from an African American director ever while holding the number one position in the box office for three weeks in a row. Incredible accomplishments for any picture, but those numbers are not the story here. The real story is the fact that Dr. Dre and Ice Cube produced the movie, which means (if you're keeping score) that the two stars made a movie about themselves—and with good reason. By being part of the production team, both Dre and Cube had the ability to portray their experiences in a way they were most comfortable with. According to *Rolling Stone*, "Ice Cube wanted the movie to show a lighter side of the group." With everything going on in Southern California, and especially in Compton (the group's hometown) at the time, the movie could have certainly taken a harsher turn, but that's not what Cube had in mind. "What's cool about the movie is that it showed how much fun we were having," he says. "We were kids, doing hip-hop and becoming famous."

What's cool to me (and *for* you) is that by taking ownership of the content and story, Cube and Dre were able to control their own brand narrative and earn money while doing it. Believe it or not, you are in a position to do the same.

The reality is that the higher you climb in your particular sport, the more networks and media outlets will request your time and ask to hear about your journey. This is for their benefit as much as, if not more than, it is yours. Your story is great content, and to the networks and media who are reaching out to you, content (especially that of the exclusive variety) is money. The more link clicks and traffic your story produces, the more dollars the outlets receive from their advertisers—zero of which goes to you. Until now.

Get your video camera out and start recording. If you're a highly recruited high school athlete, your recruiting experience is incredible content. Turn the camera on and document it. If you're a college athlete, your ability to balance school and athletics, not to mention having a social life, is incredible content. Turn the camera on and document it. If you're a rookie entering a professional sports league, your trials and tribulations make for incredible content. Turn the camera on. Take back ownership of your own story by creating your own content and managing your own narrative.

Stop waiting for the media to come to you. Take your journey to them *and* get paid for it.

$$\cdot \ \cdot \ \cdot$$

There is no better time to be an individual with aspirations of creating a brand than today. The technology is staring you right in the face as you interact and engage with it every day on your phone. The days of relying entirely on the media to cover your brand are over. The days of waiting for journalists to approach you for interviews are over. You control your story now. From hiring a film crew, to writing the script, to owning the content, the only person stopping you from building a brand is you.

- ➡ **Hire your own film crew like Sandy Lyle.**
- ➡ **Write your own script like Chris Bosh.**
- ➡ **Produce and sell your own content like Ice Cube and Dr. Dre.**

Ask yourself:

- ➡ **Am I building unique content to tell my story?**
- ➡ **What type of content would I create? What stories would I tell?**
- ➡ **Do I have a brand story worth pitching/selling to a media outlet? What is it?**

what are you doing before the game?

As suggested earlier in our Russell Westbrook example, if the rules don't allow for personal expression during the game, find your window of freedom outside of the traditional four quarters or two halves. One area of opportunity being leveraged more and more by athletes and teams is pregame, a moment in time in which key members of your target market are still watching (most notably the media) while the rules are typically much more relaxed.

catwalk

Perhaps no athlete uses the pregame window better than style enthusiast Odell Beckham, Jr., who introduces a brand-new pair of custom cleats prior to each game. From Batman-themed footwear to those paying homage to cartoon character Charlie Brown (my personal favorite), "OBJ" has cornered the pregame market. And the media eat it up. Each week during the season, without fail, Twitter will be inundated with mentions from notable bloggers and journalists reporting on the wide receiver's latest cleat creations—the ideal scenario for an athlete who is no doubt destined for a post-football career in fashion and design. According to Beckham, looking the part has always been an important element of his life and his game: "I've always liked to dress up, I've always liked to look good. You look good, you feel good, you play good." Not to mention, brand good.

By using his athletic platform as a stage (literally) to express his creativity and eye, Beckham has set himself apart from other athletes in the style department. So much so that in April of 2016, *GQ* named the New York Giants wide receiver as one of the thirteen most stylish men in the world, along with the likes of rapper Drake and actor Tom Hardy.

OBJ has turned the football field into his own personal catwalk, showing us that with a little creative thinking, an athlete can work around the rules to drive conversation and build a brand.

with my clique

I will be the first to admit that I know very little about rugby. Having grown up in the United States, my full-contact sport of choice was and is American football. But that's far from the case outside my home country, especially in New Zealand, where rugby is often regarded as the national sport. At the forefront of that popularity is the New Zealand national team, the All Blacks. The pride of New Zealand, the All Blacks are the most successful international rugby side of all time, having won 77 percent of their games since their inception in 1903.

If you know anything about the All Blacks, you know about the *haka*, "an ancient posture dance of the New Zealand Māori that," according to New Zealand's official tourism site, "was traditionally used to prepare a war party for battle." The site goes on to describe the haka as "one of the most feared and respected pre-match rituals in the world." It's hard to disagree—if for nothing else, out of fear. If you haven't seen a haka performance, I strongly recommend you hit up YouTube and take it in…with the lights on…and while in the company of others.

The haka and the athletes performing it are no joke. But it's the unique nature of the dance and the consistency with which it is performed that make it memorable. So much so that if you were to Google the words "All Blacks rugby," you would find that photos of the team performing the haka before a match significantly outnumber those of actual in-game performances. The All Blacks might be the most successful rugby side of all time, but it's the pregame haka that makes them world famous.

16 million

the number of views for a video of the All Blacks performing the haka prior to the 2011 Rugby World Cup Final

think you can dance?

Player introductions are one of the few moments in team sports that are about the individual rather than the group, which make it a great opportunity for an athlete to create a signature moment. That's what Ray Lewis did during his seventeen-year career as a middle linebacker for the Baltimore Ravens. Lewis won two Super Bowls with the franchise, but he may be best known for what he calls the "squirrel dance." That's the name of the dance Lewis performed before games as he exited the tunnel during player introductions.

According to Lewis, the dance was never meant to become the iconic identifier that it ultimately developed into. "This guy in my hometown, Kirby Lee, would always do this dance, and the dance was called the 'squirrel,' and I told him I was gonna do that dance one day." But after the home crowd lost their minds over Lewis's new pregame waltz, there was no turning back. It became part of his brand.

In 2013, after Lewis announced his intention to retire, fans, corporations, and even politicians across the country paid tribute to the thirteen-time Pro-Bowler, with each tribute connected by one common thread: the squirrel dance. Videos poured in of fans performing their own renditions of Lewis's dance, and hotels commissioned light shows on the sides of their buildings that emulated Lewis's famous jig. Not even Denver's mayor, Michael Hancock, was able to resist the urge to dance like Ray. (Okay, Hancock was forced to emulate Lewis after losing a bet with Baltimore mayor Stephanie Rawlings-Blake over the result of the Broncos-versus-Ravens playoff game that year.)

Lewis may not have planned for it, but he provides us with the gold standard of pregame introduction branding. The spotlight is there. The freedom is there. The opportunity is there.

· · ·

If one door closes, try opening another and another and another until you find one that gives you the room you need to build your brand. Whether it's pregame, postgame, or practice, find a way to use your athletic platform to make a statement.

→ **Show off your style like OBJ.**
→ **Celebrate your culture like the All Blacks.**
→ **Dance 'til you can't dance no more like Ray Lewis.**

Ask yourself:

→ **What can I do before the game to stand out and tell my story?**
→ **What makes my pregame story unique? Is it worth talking about?**
→ **How visible is my story? Can people see it from the stands? On TV?**

mad (wo)men

Have you ever noticed that professional athletes often wait until they've been traded or leave via free agency to take out their first ad (typically one thanking their now former city for the previous years of support)? What exactly are they waiting for? Surely athletes have something to say prior to their departure, right? Even though the timing seems off, I do applaud the use of paid media to convey a message. Despite being one of the most tried and true forms of communication for traditional marketers and brands, advertising is one of the least leveraged in the athlete world. That's why these ads, which you often find in local papers, garner national headlines. The scarcity of advertising makes the rare athlete-produced advertisement newsworthy.

It won't be this way for long, however, as more and more athletes recognize the opportunity and set out to build their personal brands through this medium. But for the moment, opportunity exists to use both conventional and modern forms of promotion to create separation between an individual and his or her competition.

This is your time to strike. Now that you've built a sizeable and faithful following, it's time to invest in advertising that reaches them.

pay to play

What many individuals and companies fail to realize is that users rarely see their social media posts unless those posts are supported by advertising dollars. According to Instagram, "users miss 70 percent of the posts that show up in their feeds," which means they see just "30 percent of the content" shared by accounts they follow. As Kyle Bunch, managing director of social media at advertising agency R/GA put it, "If you're not going to put money behind promoting your content, organic engagement is a real tough thing to produce sustainably."

30%

users "see just 30% of the content shared by accounts they follow" on Instagram.

Translation: if you don't pay, you don't play.

Before you invest in a social media campaign, spending dollars that may ultimately prove inefficient, build a plan of attack. Advertising should not be built in a vacuum; every ad you place or investment you make should feed off a previous ad and complement the content you are pushing out. Advertising is an art—not simply the design of the ad, but the timing and placement as well. The smarter you are about your rollout, the more effective you will be.

Consider these two paid media strategies that I've used over the course of my career, and in an ideal situation, employ them both.

keep the faucet running

The evergreen strategy is about ensuring a constant flow of investment into your social media posts. If, for twelve months out of the year, you are fueling all of your posts with paid media dollars, you have a much better chance of ending the year as the most socially talked-about athlete within your competitive set. That's a story ("Most Talked-About Short Stop" or "Most Talked-About Running Back") you can take to your next potential endorser or employer.

turn it up!

The second strategy is about turning up your investment levels in key moments—the times when the spotlight is already on you and/or the event you are participating in. In those cases, spend more than would be typical on paid media to make that light shine even brighter and take advantage of the preexisting hype around the situation. Similar to the above, by outspending your competition in these windows, there's a good chance you walk away as the most talked-about athlete during that event. Once again, that's the type of sexy story that can help you break into the industry you're most passionate about.

Don't wait until your career is over to spend money on your brand. Keep the faucet running, and when the timing is right, turn it up.

give them the Heisman

If you're looking for unique ways to promote and bring attention to your brand beyond social, look no further than your local Heisman trophy campaign. Schools pushing their star football player as a candidate for what is arguably the most prestigious individual award in college sports are focused on one thing: conversation. That's exactly what you need. The more that people—specifically the media and fans—are talking about a school's candidate, the better chance that athlete has to win. Similarly, the more that people are talking about you as an individual—specifically around the subject you're most passionate about—the more likely you are to pique the interest of brands in that space. So the next time you chuckle at the school that pays to paint a mural of their starting quarterback on a water tower in the middle of nowhere in Texas, realize that you now know that athlete's name. Then ask yourself, do the people I want thinking about me know my name? If the answer is no, go find a water tower.

waste management

In advertising there's a word used to describe promotional materials seen by those outside of a desired targeted audience. It's called *waste*, and it's something you can't afford. When working with a small budget (which will likely be the case for most of you reading this book), it's imperative that the audience you're pursuing sees the ads you purchase. Anyone else who comes across your ad is a waste of your money. One of the best ways to avoid waste is to ensure that your advertising is targeted. In other words, fish where the fish are. If you're looking to reach high school football players, it probably doesn't make sense to run an ad in the *New York Times*. There would be a lot of impressions lost on a much older audience in that campaign.

Fish where the fish are.

You can't close your eyes and hope for the best when placing ads. Be calculated and strategic with how and where you buy. The more efficient you are with your targeting, the further your dollar will go.

For an independent entrepreneur like you, one of the most effective forms of advertising comes via social media. Platforms like Facebook and Twitter provide easy-to-manage targeting tools that allow you to scale your audience up or down while focusing your campaign on those with specific interests. The better you are at targeting, the more you'll be rewarded, as if it were a game. Be deliberate and strategic before you invest your time and resources into an ad campaign. Identify your audience, recognize where they spend their time, and then meet them there. As I said, fish where the fish are.

· · ·

Once you've built your army of brand ambassadors and written a story worth reading, it's time to think about building hype through advertising. If marketing were an assembly line, advertising would be at the end of that line waiting to put a bow on the perfect moment or story. The skill comes in knowing when and where to place your bow.

athletes are brands too

- ➡ **Keep the advertising faucet running, and turn it up in key moments.**
- ➡ **Get creative in how you produce advertising; generate PR through execution.**
- ➡ **Avoid waste by targeting your advertising to a specific audience.**

Ask yourself:

- ➡ **Am I currently spending money on paid media? Why or why not?**
- ➡ **Is my current media spend worth press coverage? Can it be? How?**
- ➡ **Where can I promote my brand to a specific target, minimizing waste?**

throw shade

Let me ask you this: Prior to Conor McGregor, how many of Floyd Mayweather's opponents can you name? Despite the fact that Mayweather is often considered to be, pound for pound, the greatest boxer of all time, you can probably only name one other foe: Manny Pacquiao. Why? Because of the rivalry. Because of all the hype built up outside the ring prior to the fight. Among traditional boxers, that level of contention did not exist for Mayweather beyond Pacquiao, and the numbers show it. All of that prefight drama worked. According to *Business Insider*, the fight between the two adversaries "shattered expectations by tens of millions of dollars," thanks to a record 4.4 million pay-per-view buys.

We love rivalries, and rivalries build brands. Fans and the media can't get enough of them. Conversely, if it's not a rivalry, if there isn't a little bad blood, we don't care. Every single one of you has a rival, but we only care about a few of them. Pick one and make us care.

Work together and throw some shade.

build-a-rival

When it comes to rivalries, if one doesn't exist, create one. That's the situation Mayweather found himself in post-Pacquiao, having run through boxing opponent after boxing opponent. He was so successful and so good at what he did that it literally became boring to watch. Not even the outlandish claims he made on an almost weekly basis could stir fans or the media anymore. He was right. He *was* the best. And it really *wasn't* close. We agreed and moved on to something a little less certain, like the UFC.

Insert Conor McGregor.

Legendary WWE commentator Jim Ross described McGregor, an MMA icon, as "the perfect heel." In professional wrestling, a "heel" can be defined as a villain or bad guy that the crowd loves to hate. Ironically, what tends to happen with antiheroes like McGregor is, as they continue to have success, those fans who once hated them begin to love them with just as much fervor. From posing in front of a Lamborghini wearing nothing but underwear and sneakers to threatening to break Floyd Mayweather's face, McGregor became the Muhammad Ali of the MMA world. That's where the fun begins: two of the greatest self-promoters the world of sport has ever seen together in one epic war of words.

It started as an innocent response to a question posed to McGregor by Conan O'Brien on his talk show, in which the fighter was asked if he would ever consider fighting Mayweather in a boxing match. McGregor replied, "If you're asking would I like to fight Floyd Mayweather—I mean, who would not like to dance around the ring for $180 million?" That response ignited what would become the hottest conversation in both boxing and mixed martial arts.

This was no accident. In fact, Mayweather himself admitted to starting rumors of a potential fight between the two. "The rumors that y'all have been hearing [are] the rumors I started. It may not be a rumor." Gasoline, meet fire. We call that a *tactic* in the business. Mayweather is not simply a phenomenal boxer; he's also very much aware of the power of marketing and has used it to build his personal brand throughout his career. If he were not such a great fighter, he'd have taken my job years ago.

More so than other sports, fighting, whether that is MMA or boxing, is almost entirely about hype. When the Michigan and Ohio State football programs get together at the Big House, the hype is built in. That blood has been boiling for over a hundred years, no buildup necessary. But before McGregor answered what was nothing more than a hypothetical question posed by Conan, there was no rivalry. The idea did not exist. What you see here is the epitome of manufactured conflict, and it worked to perfection. The Mayweather-versus-McGregor story line is reality television meets the WWE.

hug-a-hater

Would you believe me if I told you that the 1979 matchup between Michigan State and Indiana State is the highest-rated NCAA men's basketball championship game of all time? It is, and you can thank the heated rivalry between Earvin "Magic" Johnson of Michigan State and Larry Bird of Indiana State for that. But the Magic-versus-Bird story didn't stop there. It's one of the fiercest conflicts in the history of the sport. The respective legends carried their disdain for each other all the way to the mountaintops of the NBA. Bird's Boston Celtics would face Magic's Los Angeles Lakers three times in the NBA Finals, with Boston winning one and Los Angeles taking the other two.

❝ When the new schedule would come out each year, I'd grab it and circle the Boston games. **❞** Magic Johnson

> **❝** The first thing I would do every morning was look at the box scores to see what Magic did. I didn't care about anything else. **❞** Larry Bird

The dichotomy between the country-born Bird and the city-dwelling Johnson offered the perfect contrast in playing styles and lifestyles. It was a story line built for the silver screen.

Converse thought so, at least. The shoe company decided to put both of the company's star endorsers into a commercial together highlighting their fierce rivalry (and of course their signature sneakers). But the important thing here is not that a commercial was made showcasing two icons; it's that both Bird and Magic *agreed* to be in an ad together. Sharing the spotlight is not always easy, but it's that decision to collaborate that serves as the real lesson here.

A rivalry is what you make of it. And what you make *of* it directly affects what you make *from* it. The Bird-versus-Magic rivalry was a commercial success thanks to the strategic decision making by each individual. The two were no doubt stars in their own right, but it's their bitter history together and their willingness to promote and bring attention to it that transformed them into legendary basketball players and legendary brands.

As author Jay Baer says in his book of the same name, hug your haters.

opposites attract

Like Magic versus Bird, the greatest sports rivalries often feel like something out of a Hollywood script driven by the push and pull between two opposites. That's no coincidence. We've been predisposed to this type of plot for generations. The good-versus-evil story line we see in folklore and modern-day theater translates to sports perhaps better than any other of our everyday realities.

TOP INDIVIDUAL SPORTS RIVALRIES

Larry Bird	1	Magic Johnson
Jack Nicklaus	2	Arnold Palmer
Bill Russell	3	Wilt Chamberlain
Rafael Nadal	4	Roger Federer
Martina Navratilova	5	Chris Evert
Wayne Gretzky	6	Mario Lemieux
David Pearson	7	Richard Petty
Serena Williams	8	Venus Williams
Muhammad Ali	9	Joe Frazier
Ted Williams	10	Joe DiMaggio

Source: Rubenstein (2010).

If you don't believe me when I say we love a good-versus-evil plot, look no further than the Rocky films, starring Sylvester Stallone as Rocky Balboa, a hardworking boxer from the wrong side of town. *Rocky IV*, in which Balboa fights the Russian terror Ivan Drago, was the second-worst reviewed of all of the Rocky films. Yet despite the poor reviews from critics (39 percent on Rotten Tomatoes), it was also the highest-grossing film in the series. In fact, it was the highest-grossing sports film, period, for twenty-four years after its release.

For Americans watching the film, Drago represented evil. But who do you think the villain would have been in the eyes of a young Russian watching the movie? My money is on Rocky. It's that divisive conflict between two flag-bearing figures that gets our juices flowing. Once again, society wants to identify with something bigger than itself. Rocky represented something more to Americans, Drago something more to Russians. They each gave people the us-versus-them model our world craves. Whether it's

Mayweather versus McGregor, Michigan versus Ohio State, or Bird versus Magic, the *Rocky IV* script has played out for over a century in sports.

When looking for a rival of your own, find your antithesis among the most popular athletes of your sport. By doing so you will have a much better chance of winning over a community looking for someone new to relate to. Find the Ivan Drago to your Rocky Balboa.

• • •

Rivalries are what sports are all about, and yet so many of today's athletes, coaches, and teams want to downplay them or ignore them entirely. While the door closes on those who choose to play it safe, a window opens to the few brave enough to stir the pot.

➡ **Create your own rivalry like Floyd Mayweather and Conor McGregor.**
➡ **Publicize your rivalry like Magic Johnson and Larry Bird.**
➡ **Find your opposite like Rocky Balboa versus Ivan Drago.**

Ask yourself:

➡ **Is there a relevant athlete that I can create a rivalry with? Who? Why?**
➡ **How am I different from my rival? Can I play up those differences?**
➡ **How can I bring attention to and publicize my rivalry?**

fight for right

Part of building a successful personal brand is having a point of view. Indifference is the death of a brand. The moment people feel nothing for a brand is the moment the brand ceases to exist. You're not a robot; you're a person, and with that humanity comes opinions and feelings and emotions.

Be thoughtful with how you express each, but express them nonetheless. Otherwise, why am I following you? Otherwise, what is there to follow at all?

There will be moments where your voice has relevance around a culturally sensitive conversation. It's your call as to whether or not you want to participate, but if you do choose to take part, be authentic and true. Show your compassion in those moments. Robots make for bad brand managers because they have no emotion for humans to empathize with. People want to feel like they're part of your life and your brand, but you have to give them something to identify with.

Now, I am not encouraging you to insert yourself into every political and sociological firestorm that comes to pass, nor am I discouraging you. What I am suggesting is that you should participate when it's genuine to you and something you believe in. I can guarantee you that if you believe in it, there is a significant population that believes in it too. And it's those people who will be with you until the end.

where there's a Williams, there's a way

While working for a company, the company's well-being supersedes your own. That's the reality. I'm not saying it's wrong, I'm not saying it's right, I'm just saying it is. Knowing that, your ability to build your brand outside of the confines of your employer becomes crucially important.

In May of 2014, NFL running back DeAngelo Williams tragically lost his mother to breast cancer. To generate awareness around the importance of testing among women, Williams looked to wear pink cleats and accessories on field throughout the season, not strictly during the month of October (the league's designated breast cancer awareness month). The NFL said no, citing the league's uniform policy.

That didn't stop Williams from generating awareness within the rules. Instead of inserting pink into his NFL-issued uniform, Williams dyed the tips of his hair, which are visible even with his helmet on. According to the NFL running back, the league is "not specific on what color it [hair] has to be."

Pink found its way onto the field, and Williams drove awareness for a cause near and dear to his heart.

> ❝ It's not just about October for me; it's not just a month; it's a lifestyle.❞
> DeAngelo Williams

Your league or governing body is often not going to support your personal endeavors, especially when those activities find their way onto the field of play. However, that doesn't mean you can't come up with ways to create conversation. As was the case in this example, there is almost always a way.

bring the noise

They called it the "Battle of the Sexes," a tennis match between female tennis star Billie Jean King and male tennis athlete and former Wimbledon champion Bobby Riggs. Riggs had previously boasted that he could, at fifty-five years old, outplay any female tennis player in the world. According to King, Riggs had been tirelessly pursuing a match with her, an offer she had repeatedly declined. That is until Riggs challenged and defeated the top-ranked female tennis player at the time, Margaret Court—a moment that convinced King to accept Riggs's challenge and carry the torch for women athletes all over the world.

The match itself will go down as one of the most, if not the most, anticipated and hyped matches in the history of the sport. This event more closely resembled a Don King–produced heavyweight title fight than a tennis exhibition. Riggs did everything he could to fuel the fire between him and his rival, not to mention reigniting the debate of equality between men and women.

At one point Riggs summed up his divisive feelings about women by saying, "The best way to handle women is to keep them pregnant and barefoot."

For King and females all over the world, the moment would prove bigger than sport. "It wasn't about tennis," she said. "It was about social change." But it was sport that provided King and the fight for equality the platform needed in a time desperate for a proof point. According to Frank Gifford, who was a commentator during the ABC telecast, "It just fit in socially with what was going on in the country, and it took off like a rocket."

> **❝ It wasn't about tennis. It was about social change. ❞** Billie Jean King

From orchestrated promotional press conferences to outlandish entrances to the court on the day of the match in which Riggs would arrive via rickshaw and King via a float adorned with ostrich feathers, the match and the individuals involved did everything they could to bring attention to the moment. And in King's case, the cause.

It worked.

On September 20, 1973, tens of millions of people watched on television and thirty thousand were in attendance (the largest crowd to ever watch a tennis match) as Billie Jean King dominated her male counterpart in three straight sets. It was a triumph that would go down as a significant marker for women's rights and equality.

Had King not taken the battle for equality to the court, there is very little chance she would have drawn the level of attention she and her constituents needed. She used her athletic talents and her athletic platform to bring light to a social injustice. She used marketing to incite change. And we're all better off for it.

hero

It goes without saying that Jackie Robinson had a tremendous impact on our country and the world in becoming the first African American to play professional baseball. By breaking through the color barrier and into one of the country's most popular sports, Robinson willingly took on the responsibility and severe criticism that would come with it. As he would say in a 1972 interview, just before his passing, Robinson was forced to endure racial slur after racial slur during his time in baseball: "You name them in terms of race and they were yelled." Despite what would break even the most strong-willed among us, Robinson displayed supreme character and fortitude throughout it all.

Those in the spotlight, as Robinson was, carry with them a heavy burden for the cause they choose to fight for, much more so than the average person. The average person is invisible and nameless to the masses. The average person can walk the streets without anticipation of being recognized. The average person is not worthy of a feature story in the *Washington Post*. But athletes and celebrities are, and because of that the load proves greater at times. As a baseball player at the highest level, Robinson would play in front of thousands on a weekly basis knowing full well what he was signing up for. As he said, "There was really too much to be done at that particular time in terms of breaking the baseball barrier to allow name calling to bother me."

It was the combination of Robinson's courage and baseball's popularity that helped bring attention to another of our country's past prejudices, and it's that combination of courage and popularity that sparked the retirement of Robinson's number forty-two jersey by all Major League Baseball teams in 1997. Today, Robinson has his own day, not because of his ability to hit a baseball or run the bases, but for his willingness to put himself at the forefront of political strife for the greater good. And it's for that reason our country will forever honor the late, great Jackie Roosevelt Robinson.

· · ·

Sports wear a variety of hats; from simple forms of entertainment to platforms from which cultural shifts can be ignited. The weight and burden carried by the games we play have more influence on our world than we sometimes realize. It's those athletes who participate in these pastimes and who do realize their significance who often create our most important movements. The reality is that we remember Billie Jean King and Jackie Robinson less for the work they did on the court and field, respectively, and more for the work they did for our world. Because of those efforts and the bravery each portrayed under fire, their names will forever be etched into the pages of our history books.

➡ **Visualize your cause like DeAngelo Williams.**
➡ **Build hype around your movement like Billie Jean King.**
➡ **Break through barriers like Jackie Robinson.**

Ask yourself:

➡ **Is there a cause I am passionate about? Does it align with my brand?**
➡ **How can I participate in supporting and bringing attention to the cause?**
➡ **What does my involvement in the cause say about my brand?**

athlete's best friend

If the media doesn't like you, no one does. For better or worse, journalists and bloggers control public opinion. People used to sarcastically say, "If it's on the internet, it *must* be true." Unfortunately, in many ways that's closer to reality than we may care to admit. If it's being reported by an even moderately credible source, most people are going to assume it to be true. This puts you as an athlete at a disadvantage—unless it doesn't. Why not take that knowledge and use it for your own gain? Why not be one of the few athletes to befriend the media rather than shut them out? Why not get the journalistic community on your side? The results can be extraordinarily rewarding for your personal brand.

the great bambino

Former New York Yankee and mythical sports figure Babe Ruth leveraged the media to create perhaps the most iconic personal brand in the history of baseball. Ruth is the definition of a sports legend, a reputation that was inflated at times and protected during others thanks to his strong relation-ship with the media. According to author Jean Shepherd in the HBO original documentary *Babe Ruth*, the media made Ruth into the stuff of folklore, saying, "Every reporter that covered Ruth had the illusion that he was a great friend of Ruth, so the minute he started writing about Ruth, he started writing about what he considered his friend." That close bond and assumed kinship kept the tabloids at bay when Ruth got into trouble off the field while garnering him front-page headlines when he found success on it.

> **❝ The media really built Babe Ruth. ❞**
> Jean Shepherd, author

Compare that to former Pittsburgh Pirate and San Francisco Giant great Barry Bonds, who had more home runs, hits, base on balls, and total bases than Ruth yet was consistently persecuted by the media thanks in part to his misgivings with the reporting community. According to Bonds, his toxic relationship with the media cost him—literally: "I kick myself now, because I'm getting great press [since being more cooperative], and I could have had a trillion more endorsements." He added, "It's on me. I'm to blame for the way I was [portrayed]."

Journalists and bloggers are used to athletes shutting them down and tuning them out, but the only people hurt in a feud between athletes and the media are the athletes themselves. Be different, stand out, and make friends among one of the most influential communities in sports and watch as your brand becomes the beneficiary of your competition's lack of cooperation.

The only people hurt in a feud between athletes and the media are the athletes.

know when to turn *off* the camera

If we're honest with ourselves, much of the criticism athletes receive from media and fans around leaked photos or videos that surface after a night of partying is hypocritical. I've never been much of a partier myself (I'm admittedly a square), but I know if I had a camera on me at all times, as these athletes often do, even I would have some pretty embarrassing college moments caught on film. The thing is, when I was going to school, I was basically invisible and Twitter didn't exist, so I was free to be young and many times stupid. But athletes live in a different world than I did when I was a teenager, and fair or not, that has to be taken into account by anyone who plans on making a career of professional athletics.

It's up to you, as the athlete and the brand. What's more important, the night out or the contract? The party or the career? The experience or the brand? I realize that decision, especially in the moment, isn't always an easy one to make. But one has to live with the consequences that come with those choices. It's the life you've selected and the responsibility you bear. I'm not here to lecture you; I'm here to help you build a brand. In many cases, being caught on camera in compromising situations can severely damage that brand.

In 2016, Laremy Tunsil came into the NFL Draft touted by most prognosticators as a top-three pick. However, just minutes before the draft started, a video of what appeared to be Tunsil smoking from a bong was posted to his Twitter account. As a result, the young offensive lineman out of the University of Mississippi slid to the Miami Dolphins at the thirteenth pick. According to Market Watch, that video may have cost Tunsil over $10 million. Ten. Million. Dollars. The fiscal ramifications alone are enough to scare anyone straight, but it's the brand I would be most concerned about. If Tunsil lives up to his billing, he will likely make up for the money he lost—amazing as that sounds. However, he will never be able to rid himself of that video. The internet does not forget, nor does our society. His brand will always carry with it the labels, true or not, born from those images.

It's not about sacrificing experiences. No one is asking you to lock yourself in your room. But there needs to be awareness and balance. It's about being smart and knowing that everything you do contributes to your brand. Your brand is like a spiderweb—anything that comes into contact with it sticks.

The internet does not forget.

take a breath

Like iconic in-game performances, memorable postgame tantrums or press conference rants can stay with a brand forever. How many times has someone in your life uttered the word *practice*, only to spark another poor impersonation of Allen Iverson at the podium saying, "Talking about practice"? Or how about the word *playoffs*—made infamous by former NFL head coach Jim Mora. Chances are one of those words has instantly transported you and your friends back in time to relive the outbursts.

The sad part is that those moments go beyond the words each spoke in the moment. Not only are we transported to those respective interviews when we hear those two words, but unfortunately for each highly acclaimed sports figure, we subconsciously go to each of those events when we hear their names. It's not just us; it's the internet as well. At the time of this writing, there is a website dedicated entirely to Mora's rant about playoffs (www.jimmoraplayoffs.com). That's when you know your tirade made it.

Incredibly, each of these instances occurred *before* YouTube, *before* Twitter, *before* Facebook. Imagine if they happened today. If a picture of a crying Michael Jordan can become one of the most popular social media memes of all time, what would happen to Iverson and Mora today?

The difference is that Jordan could not have predicted that his shedding of tears would ignite a social media feeding frenzy, but both Iverson and Mora were in control of their own behavior and their own words. Their brands were affected by their own decisions. You need to understand the impact your actions and words can have on your brand for the rest of your life, and in the heat of the moment…just take a breath.

• • •

Acknowledging and accepting the way news spreads today will benefit you and your brand. The journalistic media often starts the fire, while social media fuels it. But in most cases, these PR nightmares can be avoided altogether with a little camaraderie, foresight, and discipline.

- ➡ **Be kind to your local journalist.**
- ➡ **Know when to turn the camera off.**
- ➡ **Take a breath the next time someone asks you an absurd question.**

Ask yourself:

- ➡ **How would I describe my current relationship with the press?**
- ➡ **How can I improve or establish that relationship?**
- ➡ **Do I have media allies? Who?**

only if you love it

During my career I've seen too many athletes sign with brands simply for the money rather than the love of the product they are hired to endorse. Under those circumstances these individuals are often caught wearing competitive merchandise, which results in a public relations firestorm for both the athlete and the company that hired them. If in one breath you're telling your fans that you love a product but in the next breath you are seen wearing a competitor's brand, what do you think that does for your credibility? It hurts. It hurts your chances of convincing an audience that what you say is genuine, which ultimately makes it much more difficult for you to establish a credible brand. It also hurts your chances of getting a deal from future endorsers, regardless of industry, based on your resulting reputation. If you're going to sign an endorsement deal with a company, make sure you absolutely love the product you're signing up to recommend or risk permanently scarring your personal brand.

brand it like Beckham

Known as much for his supreme style and looks as for his outstanding soccer skills, David Beckham was able to build a bridge for his brand that transcended sports. According to Beckham, his aptitude for the aesthetic started at a young age: "Even as a kid, 7 or 8 years old, I liked to wear nice shoes. I liked to wear a nice suit my mum or dad bought me."

By leveraging his natural-born love for fashion and his reputation for being one of the most attractive people in the world (in 2015, *People* magazine named him "The Sexiest Man Alive"), Beckham built a personal brand that led to endorsement deals with the likes of adidas and clothing retailer H&M. Those brand collaborations, coupled with the media coverage that surrounded him everywhere he went, only fueled his reputation as a style icon. In response to his retirement in 2013, *GQ* went so far as to write a feature that celebrated his "indisputable status as a first-ballot style hall of famer."

Beckham was so successful in building his brand on and off the field that in 2015, two years after his retirement from the game, Beckham banked his largest earnings ever by bringing in $75 million.

FIND **COMMON GROUND** BETWEEN YOUR BRAND AND THEIRS

YOUR BRAND   **OUR** BRAND   **MY** BRAND

big fish, small pond

The concept isn't hard to understand. The biggest fish in the smallest ponds stand out, and everyone wants a piece of them. The same holds true for athletes. Coming out of school, athletes will often be courted by multiple brands within a given industry, leaving a young and inexperienced adult with a very big business decision to make. Provided the option of two strong, competent brands—one with a roster of what can sometimes be hundreds of athletes from a given sport and another brand with a fraction of that—I would recommend to my client to join the second brand just about every time.

A brand that needs you is a brand that will work hard for you.

At the end of the day, signing to an organization with a laundry list of stars is going to make it much more difficult for you to receive the type of brand support and attention you believe you deserve. Every company is working within the boundaries of its budget, which means not every product and not every athlete will get resourced. Going to an equally recognizable brand that happens to have a shorter roster of athletes will require much less time and effort to rise to the top of the priority list.

A brand that needs you is a brand that will work hard for you.

participate

I hear it all the time when presenting promotional opportunities to athletes: "I just want to play (insert sport)." I get it; you love the game you play, and that's all that matters to you. I can relate; if I had it my way, I would just write. Forget speaking at conferences, doing interviews, or networking. Give me a computer, a coffee shop, and a protein bar, and I'm happy. But then you wouldn't care about what I had to say. My writing would never leave my computer. No one would know who I am. In order to build a brand, you have to participate.

athletes are brands too

When you sign on to endorse a product or a company, participate. Not for the company, but for you. In most cases you're talking about multi-million-dollar organizations that have the ability to get your message out in ways you can't. But that only happens if you participate.

Endorsement deals are not about the money (though in some sports, it is significant); it's about the exposure and storytelling that comes with that partnership. If you are great at what you do and manage your brand effectively, you will make the money. You will have multiple lucrative offers to choose from. Select the partner that best aligns with the brand you want to build, and squeeze everything you can out of them. They'll embrace it. Trust me, I've been on the other side. I want my athletes to ask for *more*. I want my athletes to present content and storytelling ideas to *me*. I want my athletes to *participate*. In return, I will do everything I can to make them famous and to build their brand.

I can't tell you how many times I've sat in a room talking to counterparts about a potential campaign that called for an athlete to play a starring role and during that conversation a particular player was written off because of the individual's unwillingness to participate. In those situations it's not the company that's hurt. If one athlete says no, there are several others who will say yes.

The only person hurt by their lack of participation is the athlete.

• • •

Money should not be the deciding factor of an endorsement deal. If you manage your brand correctly, the dollars will come. Stay true to yourself and the brand you want to portray. If you love the product or industry you align with and find a partner willing to invest in you, you'll love putting in the work that comes with the relationship.

- ➡ Choose the sponsor and industry that best aligns with your personal brand.
- ➡ Find a partner that's willing to invest in building your brand, not just theirs.
- ➡ Participate!

Ask yourself:

- ➡ Which industry best aligns with my brand? Which companies?
- ➡ How many similar endorsers do those companies currently have?
- ➡ What can I bring to any of those companies that helps their brand and mine?

be ready

There will be favorable times in your career where you become the subject of local, regional, or even national conversation. It could be around your commitment to a school, an extraordinary performance in a game, or your part in winning a title. The time will come when people are singing your praises and you're trending. While all of that conversation is free of charge and organic, that does not mean it's time to close your wallet or slow down on your content releases. It's just the opposite, in fact. Strike while the iron is hot. Take advantage of the excitement around your brand to create even more buzz, except this time focus on the part of your story that really matters to you personally. The part of the story no one knows about.

Do you play an instrument? Is music your true love? Do you plan on diving into songwriting full-time after your athletic career is up? Now is the time to tell the world. Show people who you are underneath the uniform. With your success comes a public that's more willing to lend an ear. When they do, you need to be ready to tell that untold story. It's these moments when you reach your highest levels of success in sports that will set you up for your greatest levels of influence outside of it.

But only if you're ready.

In the industry the phrase we use is *planned reactive*, meaning having content and budget prepared for moments that we anticipate *might* happen. What are we going to do if one of our athletes wins the MVP award? We're ready with content and money to invest. What are we going to do if our school wins the national championship? We're ready with content and money to invest.

What are *you* going to do if *you* win the MVP award? What happens if *you* win the national championship? For most of you, the answer is nothing—not unless the media chooses to write a story about you or your school or a partner chooses to invest in you. Forget that. Flip the script and write your own story. Be ready with your own content. Carve out your own budget, and buy your own advertising.

Shifting the conversation is much easier than creating it. But your window to shift people's attention from on field to off is a small one. You have to be ready.

objective #3: crash the biggest parties

If I was to be known for a single marketing expression and philosophy, I hope it would be this: "It's easier to crash a party than throw a party." It's a concept I've used throughout my career, across multiple industries and most recently within sports. It's my favorite part of the job and happens to represent our third and final objective: to be the most talked-about brand during the most important moments of your industry or sport.

The idea is as simple as it sounds: stop wasting your energy trying to bring people to your party; instead, focus on disrupting someone else's. Think about it. What takes less time, money, and effort, throwing your own party or doing something disruptive and memorable at someone else's? I can tell you from experience, it's the second one.

> **❝ It's easier to crash a party than throw a party. ❞** Jeremy Darlow

the formula

It's not enough to simply say it's easier to crash a party. To truly equip you with the tools you need, a system must be developed, shared, and followed. That brings us to the party-crashing formula.

I've always been a fan of incorporating science into marketing. Once you discover a successful method for brand development and promotion, there's less time spent inventing and more time spent improving. If you have a proven formula to follow, from there it's simply about trial and error and discovering which combinations work the best. That's the case with the theory behind party crashing.

To effectively crash a party, you need three things: an event of mass scale, a disruptive story, and key influencers. It's the combination of the three that will bring your brand to the forefront of the conversation and have you leaving the event with the coveted "life of the party" label.

Let's break down each component.

the biggest parties

First, what do I mean by party? In marketing terms, a party is *an event or moment of mass scale*, emphasis here being on the words *mass scale*. If you truly want to make noise, you need to crash moments with the biggest audiences. As it relates to sports, the benchmark parties are events like the NCAA men's basketball national championship (the 2016 final averaged 17.8 million viewers), the FIFA Women's World Cup (the 2015 final averaged 25.4 million viewers), and the Super Bowl (the 2016 Super Bowl averaged a staggering 111.9 million viewers). Of course not everyone reading this book will have the opportunity to participate in events like these, but in each of your cases, there exists an equivalent within your world. Your national championship game may be the yearly matchup between you and your crosstown rival. Your World Cup may be the one nationally televised game of your year. Your Super Bowl may be your postseason finale, regardless of how far you go. Bottom line: the bigger the party you crash, the more noise you can make. Find your moments to turn heads.

	Sport	Event	US Viewers (in millions)
TOP 2016 EVENTS BY LEAGUE/SPORT	NFL	**Broncos/Panthers** (Super Bowl)	**111.86**
	MLB	**Cubs/Indians** (World Series, Game 7)	**40.05**
	Olympics	**Primetime Coverage** (Night Four)	**33.44**
	NBA	**Cavaliers/Warriors** (NBA Finals, Game 7)	**31.02**
	CFB	**Alabama/Clemson** (National Championship)	**26.18**
	CBB (M)	**Villanova/North Carolina** (National Championship)	**17.75**
	Soccer	**Chile/Argentina** (Copa América Final)	**9.8**
	NHL	**Penguins/Sharks** (Stanley Cup Final Game 6)	**5.41**
	CBB (W)	**UConn/Syracuse** (National Championship)	**2.97**
	Tennis (M)	**Serena Williams/Angelique Kerber** (Wimbledon Final)	**2.21**

Source: Paulsen (2017).

the boldest stories

Second, how does one crash a party? I define *party crashing* as inserting a brand into an existing event through a disruptive and relevant activation. The focus here being on the words *disruptive* and *relevant*. If you're going to truly crash a party, you need to interrupt the regularly scheduled programming by doing something unexpected and jarring, so much so that viewers turn their attention (and their tweets) away from the event itself and instead focus on you and your brand. Behind that disruption needs to be a story relevant to the situation and authentic to the brand delivering it (that's you). This is where the most strategic of marketing storytellers excel. Be bold, brave, and loud, and your brand will be rewarded with conversation, acclaim, and exposure.

athletes are brands too

the coolest people

Finally, in order for a brand activation to gain traction, it needs influencers backing it. By influencers I mean the tastemakers within a community or industry that inspire action among those aforementioned masses. The brands that are able to engage this elite segment of their target population with the right story during the right moment set off a chain reaction that drives more clicks, more tweets, and more headlines around the brand's chosen narrative. Lucky for some of you, you already are influencers, which means this portion of your job is done. You *are* the cool kid.

For those of you who are on your way but not quite there yet, this is where building your network comes into play. The more influential the friends you have supporting you are, the better chance you have of effectively crashing a party.

THE FORMULA:

BIG PARTY
+ BOLD STORY
+ COOL KIDS

PARTY CRASHED

The gold standard in party crashing comes from Ellen DeGeneres's star-studded selfie at the 2014 Oscars, sponsored by Samsung and orchestrated to drive awareness around their newest phone. Ellen stopped the show, walked into the crowd, and took a selfie with Hollywood's elite. One expert valued the stunt at between a staggering $800 million and $1 billion. Samsung would have never generated that level of value from an event they themselves built from the ground up.

The company executed the formula perfectly by leveraging an existing moment of mass scale (the 2014 Oscars averaged 43 million viewers), inserting the brand in a disruptive and relevant way (taking a selfie in the middle of the show), and pushing their message out through the lens of influencers (Ellen and her Hollywood A-list friends).

Not only did Ellen's selfie steal the show, it nearly broke the internet by becoming (at the time) the most retweeted tweet of all time. Party officially crashed. Learn from Samsung: stop spending your time throwing parties and start crashing them. Your brand (and wallet) will thank you.

Now let's take a look at some other well-known party crashers within sports and identify what made each successful.

call your shot

After coming up short in the 1992 Olympic games, track star Michael Johnson was on a mission to leave the 1996 games a legend. And that he did, but not for the reasons you would think. Johnson came into the 200 m and 400 m dash events that year as a favorite to win gold, something he would go on to accomplish in world-record fashion. But it's the gold he wore on his feet that left the most lasting impression. It doesn't matter what generation you're from, if you are remotely interested in track and field, you know about Michael Johnson and his Olympic gold spikes.

In what might be my favorite example of an athlete crashing a party, Johnson nailed every element of the formula. As an influencer, Johnson chose one of the most important moments in track and field to make a statement. Party crashing starts with scale and ends with the story, and there is no bigger stage than the Olympics, no bolder statement than wearing gold spikes during an event in which you are favored to win. Johnson wasn't about to back down from the pressure that came with those expectations. Quite the contrary. By wearing gold spikes, Johnson let it be known that he fully expected to win the matching gold medals he trained so hard to earn. He called his shot. And with that bravado, he became a legend.

Had Johnson pulled this stunt off at the world indoors or the trials leading up to the games, no one would have known. No one would have cared. Right athlete. Right moment. Right story. Legend.

> **EVENT:** 1996 Olympics
> **MOMENT:** Michael Johnson Calls His Shot, Wears Gold Spikes
> **INFLUENCER:** Michael Johnson

make a (fashion) statement

As was the case for James Harden and Shaun White, former Ohio State running back Ezekiel Elliott became known as much for his physical features as for his on-field performance. Elliott made a name for himself by being one of the fiercest competitors in the sport, but his brand differentiator came to be his propensity to wear his jersey in such a way that highlighted his "assets"; in this case, his abdominal muscles. I'm pretty sure he had more than the six-pack typical for the average human. On field, Elliott would wear his jersey like a crop top, exposing those now-famous abs, which the NCAA would later take exception to, ultimately establishing what could be affectionately known as the "Ezekiel Elliott Rule." It states that players wearing "jerseys tucked under the shoulder pads or exposed back pads" will be forced to vacate the field for at least one play.

Not surprisingly, once this new rule hit the newswires, reporters from every major sporting news outlet tied the story back to Elliott. But with conflict comes exposure and opportunity for brands to make a statement. Elliott took a stance against the rule, calling it "silly" and signing a petition to protest. Whether he knew it at the time or not, Elliott was building his brand identity around his abdominal muscles.

It's what Elliott did at the NFL Draft after the NCAA enacted the jersey rule that should serve as a lesson to every hopeful party crasher reading this book. The "hero in a half-shirt" (a phrase Elliott has since trademarked) crashed the NFL Draft party by wearing a buttoned up shirt…made into a crop top. I imagine it was the first of its kind (I can't confirm that, but I've never seen it before, nor do I expect to see it again). The stunt put the spotlight back on Elliott's most prominent brand identifier and subsequently created such a stir that Twitter made it a "Twitter Moment"—a feature the company sells as the place to go for "the biggest stories in the world, no matter where you are." Where we were: the NFL Draft. The story: Ezekiel Elliott's abs.

Brand built. Party crashed.

EVENT: NFL Draft
MOMENT: Ezekiel Elliott Wears a Half Shirt to the NFL Draft
INFLUENCER: Ezekiel Elliott

celebrate!

If you don't know who Brandi Chastain is by name alone, I bet you know her by her legendary celebration. *Sports Illustrated* anointed it as "the most memorable goal celebration in U.S. soccer history."

Let's set the scene. It's the 1999 FIFA Women's World Cup final. The heat is on, both metaphorically and literally, in a packed Rose Bowl Stadium in Los Angeles. The US women are taking on China, tied 4–4, one penalty kick away from potentially deciding the fate of the two nations. Brandi Chastain is up. If she scores, the US women win the World Cup. This is the moment every young soccer player grows up fantasizing about in his or her backyard.

With the weight of the US Women's National Team on her shoulders, Chastain scored, and in doing so won the World Cup for her team and her country.

Incredibly, had she not done what she did *after* she scored, there's a very good chance you would know neither her name nor her story. After Chastain scored, she took her jersey off, whipped it around her head, and in one of the most iconic moments in American sports history, dropped to her knees, pumped her fists, and screamed in triumph. After the match, that single image made its way to the covers of *Newsweek*, *Sports Illustrated*, and *Time*.

Something else happened in that moment. Because of that celebration, Chastain became a brand. We know who she is, not for the goal or even her career, but for the celebration. As an athlete, you can look at that as misguided or unfortunate. But as a brand marketer or an individual looking to establish his or her brand post-athletics, that should be seen as a lesson.

Every second on the field, court, or diamond counts. If the event is big enough, you can change your brand forever in an instant. No matter your sport, no matter your role on the team, no matter your history up until that point. With a single celebration, Chastain crashed one of the biggest parties in sports and secured her place as one of the most beloved athletes in US sports history.

EVENT: FIFA Women's World Cup
MOMENT: Brandi Chastain's Shirtless Celebration
INFLUENCER: Brandi Chastain

protest peacefully

For generations, peaceful protests have proven to have a place in our society, as well as in marketing. If you're looking to create conversation, then using your athletic platform to make a constructive statement is one way of doing so. That's what professional track athlete Nick Symmonds did prior to the 2012 Olympics. In the weeks leading up to the games, Symmonds sold advertising space on his left shoulder to the highest bidder. The stunt not only earned him over $11,000 but also generated tremendous media coverage around an issue important to him: the right to represent and manage one's own endorsements during the event. It was a brilliant move by a clearly savvy individual—and one I would lean on if and when you choose to take a stand and speak out against something you see as unjust.

In these moments, there are a couple of things that matter to your cause and to your brand. First, if you're going to make a statement, make sure you do it in a way that is in line with how you've carried yourself up to that point and stays true to what you want your brand to represent. If it's inauthentic, the message will get lost behind a lack of symmetry between you and the stunt, and the effort will fall flat.

Second, pick your moment carefully. Had Symmonds not made it to the 2012 Olympic games and used it as a stage to speak from, we may well have never heard about it. Nor would it have made its way into the *New York Times* in July of 2012. The moment elevates the activation.

One more reason I love this story: Nick Symmonds went to a small Division III school in Salem, Oregon, called Willamette University. You've probably never heard of it. Prior to this stunt, you had probably never heard of Nick Symmonds. The lesson here is that it doesn't matter what school you go to or how much hype you have going into an event; there's always a way to create conversation and build a brand.

lighten the mood

In 1991, a little-known rookie out of Jacksonville by the name of Dee Brown crashed the NBA Slam Dunk Contest and inserted his name into basketball lore. In a year in which former Seattle SuperSonic (and the favorite to win) Shawn Kemp would make his first appearance in the event, the Boston Celtics' six-foot-one point guard outshined his rival by infusing personality and charisma into a contest known more for the intense rivalry between Hall of Famers Michael Jordan and Dominique Wilkins than lightheartedness. But Brown didn't have the cachet afforded to those who preceded him; he needed to find another way to get people's attention. He chose charm, and it worked.

Before his first dunk attempt (and while much of the audience likely scrambled to figure who exactly Dee Brown was), Brown casually bent over and pumped air into his Reebok Pump shoes through the mechanism built into the shoe's tongue. It was a new technology for the company and no doubt a new concept to many of the fans who watched as a shoe war unfolded in front of their very eyes. According to Brown, the stunt was so disruptive and unexpected that it actually caught the attention of "His Airness," Michael Jordan, a former slam-dunk champion himself. Outside an after-party that night, he would run into Jordan, who, according to Brown, had this to say: "You did a great job out there, young fella. Nice show you put on. But, you know you started the shoe wars."

The war didn't last long.

Brown would go on to win the dunk contest, and Reebok ended up selling 6 million pairs of Pumps by the end of 1992. But both soon lost that momentum, and each fell to their foes in one way or another. The duo may have faded into obscurity completely if not for that memorable night in 1991 when Brown crashed the NBA's party. He tried something new on a big stage, and it worked. Because of the playful manner in which he introduced himself to a nationally televised audience, we will always remember that time Dee Brown won the dunk contest.

EVENT: NBA Slam Dunk Contest
MOMENT: Dee Brown Pumping Up His Reeboks Pre-Dunk
INFLUENCER: Dee Brown

try something new

I have been fortunate to manage some incredible projects and to partner with some amazing athletes and entertainers over my years in the industry. But one of my all-time favorite endeavors was the launching of the first Yeezy football cleat in the fall of 2016. It was a beautifully designed piece of footwear that emulated the wildly popular Kanye West sneaker that had taken the industry by storm a year prior on its way to being named Shoe of the Year by *Footwear News*.

Our team knew full well that the football cleat equivalent could be the biggest product introduction the sport had ever seen, and it didn't disappoint. We launched the 750 version of the cleat by way of All-Pro linebacker Von Miller during the first game of the regular season, a Thursday Night Football affair between Miller's Broncos and the team they beat the previous year in the Super Bowl, the Carolina Panthers. This was the party every football fan had been waiting for since the final whistle blew ending the 2015–2016 season.

The instant Miller stepped onto the field (in pregame, no less) wearing the never-before-seen Yeezy cleats, Twitter blew up, as did the journalist community. Every news headline across both sports and culture outlets referenced Miller and his cleats. Thursday night was ours.

But we weren't done. Three days later, we unveiled the Yeezy 350 Cleat on Adrian Peterson, Eric Berry, and DeAndre Hopkins. The headlines started flooding in once again, including SB Nation commemorating a milestone moment for the brand and one of its valued athlete partners: "Houston Texans receiver DeAndre Hopkins made history on Sunday when he scored the first touchdown of the season in a pair of Yeezy cleats from rapper Kanye West." Sunday was ours too.

We had dominated the conversation during the first week of the season by introducing a new, highly sought-after, and completely unexpected product during one of the biggest parties of the NFL regular season. First looks are always of value to the media and to fans. The more often you are able to introduce a new idea during a key culture moment, the more likely you are to own the discussion.

A new product combined with a culture moment equaled another party crashed. Week one was ours.

EVENT: NFL Week One
MOMENT: Unveiling the First Yeezy Football Cleat
INFLUENCER: Multiple NFL Athletes

• • •

Party crashing is all about timing. You can have one of the most interesting, disruptive, and newsworthy stories at your disposal, but if you go out at the wrong moment, it may very well fade into the night without anyone caring. No one remembers Michael Johnson's gold cleats without the Olympics. No one remembers Brandi Chastain's celebration without the World Cup. And no one remembers Dee Brown and his Reebok Pumps without the nationally televised NBA Slam Dunk Contest. Pick your moment, write your story, and cement your legacy.

Ask yourself:

➡ **What parties can I crash? How big are the audiences of each?**
➡ **What can I do to crash the party? Is it authentic to my brand?**
➡ **Who within my network can help me spread the word during the party?**

CONSISTENCY + FREQUENCY

BRAND RECALL

BUT BEFORE YOU START TALKING...

DRAW A MAP.

YEARLY OBJECTIVES WILL KEEP YOU ON TRACK.

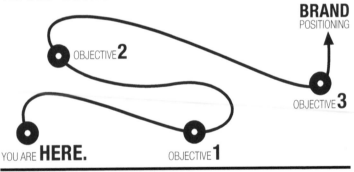

BRAND POSITIONING

OBJECTIVE **2**

OBJECTIVE **3**

YOU ARE **HERE.**

OBJECTIVE **1**

BEGIN BY ACCOMPLISHING THESE 3 OBJECTIVES:

BUILD A VISUAL **IDENTITY** | CREATE THE MOST **CONVERSATION** | CRASH THE BIGGEST **PARTIES**

1 CHOOSE YOUR...

- **LOOK**
- COLOR
- **NICKNAME**

- MOTTO
- **EMOJI**
- SIGNAL

- **CAR**
- OUTFIT
- **PLATFORM**

2 GET 'EM TALKING

7

DAYS A
WEEK

52

WEEKS A
YEAR

365

DAYS A
YEAR

3 CRASH THE PARTY

(BIG **PARTY**) + (BOLD **STORY**) + (COOL **KIDS**) = **PARTY** CRASHED

athletes are brands too

conclusion: don't live scared

Over my career and life, I've had certain wisdoms passed down to me from people I admire. One of the insights that I'll always carry with me, suggested by a former colleague, is to not "live scared." But we do. We all do. We're scared of the unknown. Of trying new things. Of taking risks. Unfortunately, those also happen to be surefire tendencies that can kill a brand.

Marketing isn't math. There's no right or wrong answer. There's no black or white. It's never that clear. There's black, gray, light gray, lighter gray, off-white, and white. Marketing is nothing but shades. Sometimes things work to perfection, but more often than not, they don't. And that's okay. It's the expectation of perfection that equates to a brand's kryptonite. Perfection breeds bland, safe, and lifeless execution. Perfection breeds the fear, insecurity, anxiety, and apprehension we're surrounded by every day. Perfection breeds failure.

Too many brands get so big that their scale becomes poisonous to the creative blood that ran through their veins and got them to that size in the first place. While those brands try to rid themselves of this self-inflicted toxin, the smaller brands with less to lose and nothing to fear are catching them. This scene

Safe is the riskiest play of them all.

plays out every day and in every aspect of our lives. Work. Relationships. Sports. You're living out this scene right now, whether you realize it or not.

The only question is, which side are you on? Scared or brave? Timid or bold?

By reading this book and investing in your own education, I can tell you with certainty that you've taken a step in the right direction and distanced yourself from the competition. This is the road less traveled. While the majority of athletes wait for others to determine their brand destiny, you've taken control of yours.

This is what you've been building toward, and now is the time when you put your newfound knowledge base to work and start constructing a brand and future of your own. This book will act as your road map along the way. When you feel lost (and you will; we all lose track of our brands at times), refer back to these pages and remember the three keys to personal brand development:

1. YOUR WINDOW

By now you see that as an athlete, you are an influencer, regardless of where you stand in your athletic career. But that authority won't last long. What you do within your window of influence can determine the trajectory of your life after sports. Your time to act is now.

2. YOUR STORY

By now you acknowledge that your brand is nothing more than a story, and you are the author. Every day you're writing a new page. It's up to you to ensure that the story is authentic to you while at the same time being unlike anything your audience has read before. Your story is your brand.

3. YOUR VOICE

By now you accept that the key to your story sticking in the minds of the public is a combination of consistency and frequency. Tell me the same story (consistency) over and over again (frequency). Only then will I be equipped to remember it and preach it to my friends. Your voice creates the conversation.

Knowledge remains the greatest equalizer of them all. From this day forward, your brand has no limits, only areas of opportunity, mountains to conquer, and Goliaths to slay. Show me a small budget, and I'll show you less pressure and more room to take risks. Show me an injury, and I'll show you a redemption story. Show me an athlete, and I'll show you a brand.

final words

I'm of the firm belief that marketers have the ability to change the world. That the individuals who have learned to understand the human mind perhaps better than anyone can use that power for good rather than to simply promote consumerism. That's not to say that commercials pushing the next great theme park or hamburger meal are bad. Who am I to judge? But I know that there are some things we would all like to fix in this world, and I know that there are people who need help.

This book is an attempt to use my education for good and to use the knowledge that has been passed down to me to help those who were not blessed with the same opportunities. I love what I do. I love to build brands. I loved writing this book.

Where you go from here is up to you. My hope is that as you implement what you have learned in these pages to build your own brand—and by doing so build your influence on our world—you will use that influence to promote progress. Hopefully by now you recognize the impact you can have on our culture.

You have been gifted with a microphone to the world. You speak and we listen. Now the only question is, what do you want us to hear?

thank you

I want to thank all of my friends and family who have supported and encouraged me throughout the process of writing this book. I can't imagine doing any of this without you.

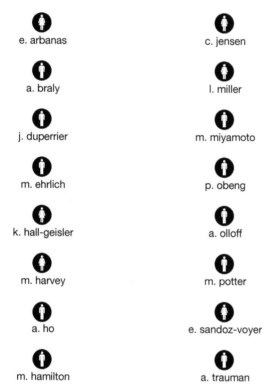

e. arbanas

a. braly

j. duperrier

m. ehrlich

k. hall-geisler

m. harvey

a. ho

m. hamilton

b. hughes

c. jensen

l. miller

m. miyamoto

p. obeng

a. olloff

m. potter

e. sandoz-voyer

a. trauman

athletes are brands too

bibliography

Ahern, Sarah. "Chicken Nugget Tweet Beats Ellen DeGeneres' Oscar Selfie to Become Most Retweeted of All Time." *Variety*, May 9, 2017. http://variety.com/2017/digital/news/chicken-nugget-tweet-most-retweeted-ellen-oscar-selfie-1202421699/.

Ahn, Jeanie. "Former NBA Star Antoine Walker: Life after Losing $110 Million." Yahoo! Finance, December 5, 2014. https://finance.yahoo.com/news/former-nba-star-antoine-walker--life-after-losing--110-million-214644672.html.

All Blacks. "The Team." Accessed November 8, 2017. http://www.allblacks.com/Teams.

Alvarez, Jose. "Journalists, Celebrities, Athletes Make Up Most of Twitter's 'Verified' List." DigitalTrends.com, June 9, 2015. https://www.digitaltrends.com/social-media/journalists-celebrities-athletes-make-up-most-of-twitters-verified-list/.

Amick, Sam. "Damian Lillard Tries to 'Paint a Picture' in Rap Career." *USA Today*, March 2, 2015. https://www.usatoday.com/story/sports/nba/blazers/2015/03/02/damian-lillard-rap-career-portland-trailblazers-terry-stotts/24275949/.

— — —. "James Harden Agrees to $200 Million Shoe Contract with adidas." *USA Today*, August 13, 2015. https://www.usatoday.com/story/sports/nba/rockets/2015/08/13/james-harden-adidas-shoe-contract/31634809/.

Araton, Harvey. "Remembering King James, before and after His Crowning." *New York Times*, June 16, 2015. https://www.nytimes.com/2015/06/17/sports/basketball/remembering-king-james-before-and-after-his-crowning.html.

Arruda, William. "16 Ways to Use Color to Bolster Your Personal Brand." *Forbes*, August 12, 2013. https://www.forbes.com/sites/williamarruda /2013/08/12/16-ways-to-use-color-to-bolster-your-personal-brand /#3ff843c88026.

Ault, Susanne. "Survey: YouTube Stars More Popular than Mainstream Celebs among U.S. Teens." *Variety*, August 5, 2014. http://variety .com/2014/digital/news/survey-youtube-stars-more-popular-than -mainstream-celebs-among-u-s-teens-1201275245/.

Badenhausen, Kurt. "David Beckham Banks His Biggest Year Ever with Earnings of $75 Million." *Forbes*, March 11, 2015. https://www.forbes .com/sites/kurtbadenhausen/2015/03/11/david-beckham-banks-his -bigger-year-ever-with-earnings-of-75-million/#4c35ac655775.

Battaglio, Stephen, and Meg James. "Super Bowl's TV Ratings Slip for the Second Straight Year." *Los Angeles Times*, February 6, 2017. http://www .latimes.com/business/hollywood/la-fi-ct-super-bowl-ratings-20170206 -story.html.

Berger, Jonah. *Contagious: Why Things Catch On*. New York: Simon & Schuster, 2016.

Berry, Ben, Nick Engvall, and Russ Bengtson. "The Complete History of Nike LeBron Sneakers Worn by King James." Complex.com, September 5, 2013. http://www.complex.com/sneakers/2013/09/lebron-james -complete-signature-sneaker-history/.

Bertoni, Steven. "Amex Reveals Details about Its Secretive Centurion Card." *Forbes*, January 25, 2011. https://www.forbes.com/sites/stevenbertoni /2011/01/25/amex-reveals-details-about-its-secretive-centurion -card/#21ce4ac82ff2.

Bilmes, Alex. "Jay-Z on His Music, Politics and His Violent Past." *GQ*, June 28, 2017. http://www.gq-magazine.co.uk/article/jay-z-interview-music -politics-violence.

athletes are brands too

Birdsong, Nick. "Did Marshawn Lynch Just Announce His Retirement on Twitter?" SportingNews.com, February 7, 2016. http://www.sportingnews.com/nfl/news/marshawn-lynch-retires-seahawks-russell-wilson-cleats-hangs-up-beastmode/1te5l6pqog4un1bi0ikde5xrvt.

Bogues, Muggsy. "How I Became 'Muggsy.'" Players' Tribune, November 16, 2015. https://www.theplayerstribune.com/muggsy-bogues-nickname/.

Bolt, Usain (@usainbolt). "Fast knows fast." Instagram photo, October 15, 2015. https://www.instagram.com/p/83yoxHocT_/.

Borruto, Ana. "Casey Neistat Disrupts Traditional Filmmaking at the Oscars." *Resource*. February 27, 2017. http://resourcemagonline.com/2017/02/casey-neistat-disrupts-traditional-filmmaking-at-the-oscars/76482/.

Brachmann, Steve. "Cowboys' Prescott and Elliott in Hunt for the Super Bowl and US Trademark Registration." IPWatchdog.com, January 12, 2017. http://www.ipwatchdog.com/2017/01/12/cowboys-prescott-elliott-super-bowl-trademark-registration/id=76627/.

Bradley, Jeff. "Shot of Redemption." *Sports Illustrated*. https://www.si.com/longform/soccer-goals/goal6.html.

Brooks, David. "When Cultures Shift." *New York Times*, April 17, 2015. https://www.nytimes.com/2015/04/17/opinion/david-brooks-when-cultures-shift.html.

Bulman, May. "Muhammad Ali: The Boxing Icon's 10 Best Quotes." *Independent*, June 4, 2016. http://www.independent.co.uk/news/people/muhammad-ali-quotes-dead-death-boxing-icon-float-like-butterfly-inspirational-a7065326.html.

Celebrity Net Worth. "Danica Patrick Net Worth." https://www.celebritynetworth.com/richest-athletes/race-car-drivers/danica-patrick-net-worth/.

Chapin, Angelina. "Four Decades after the Battle of the Sexes, the Fight for Equality Goes On." *Guardian*, March 11, 2017. https://www.theguardian.com/sport/2017/mar/11/billie-jean-king-battle-of-the-sexes-tennis.

Chiari, Mike. "Barry Bonds Comments on Portrayal by Media, Playing Career, More." BleacherReport.com, June 1, 2016. http://bleacherreport.com/articles/2643641-barry-bonds-comments-on-portrayal-by-media-playing-career-more.

Christian, Scott. "David Beckham's 25 Most Stylish Looks." *GQ*. http://www.gq.com/gallery/25-most-stylish-david-beckham-looks.

Ciotti, Gregory. "The Psychology of Color in Marketing and Branding." *Entrepreneur*, April 13, 2017. https://www.entrepreneur.com/article/233843.

Collins, Paul. "Brand Bale! Spurs Forward Follows Beckham and Ronaldo after Trademarking 'Eleven of Hearts' Goal Celebration." *Daily Mail*, June 17, 2013. http://www.dailymail.co.uk/sport/football/article-2343017/Gareth-Bale-trademarks-hearts-goal-celebration.html.

Cook, Jaylyn. "Kanye West Is a Genius, and None of Us Are Worthy of Him." Fansided.com, August 28, 2016. http://fansided.com/2016/08/28/kanye-west-genius-none-of-us-are-worthy-vmas/.

Constine, Josh. "Intagram Stories Hits 150M Daily Users, Launches Skippable Ads." TechCrunch, January 11, 2017. https://techcrunch.com/2017/01/11/instagram-stories-hits-150m-daily-users-launches-skippable-ads/.

Corben, Billy, dir. "Broke." *30 for 30.* Aired October 2, 2012, on ESPN. http://www.espn.com/30for30/film?page=broke.

Crompton, Sarah. "*Battle of the Sexes* Documentary Shows How One Fight Remains in Billie Jean King's Quest for Equality." *Telegraph*, June 12, 2013. http://www.telegraph.co.uk/sport/tennis/10113888/Battle-of-the-Sexes-documentary-shows-how-one-fight-remains-in-Billie-Jean-Kings-quest-for-equality.html.

Dr. Seuss. *Happy Birthday to You!* New York: Random House Children's Books, 1976.

Dua, Tanya. "Emojis by the Numbers: A Digiday Data Dump." Digiday.com, May 7, 2015. https://digiday.com/marketing/digiday-guide-things-emoji/.

"Ellen's Oscar Selfie: Worth $1 Billion?" NBC News, April 9, 2014. http://www.nbcnews.com/tech/social-media/ellens-oscar-selfie-worth-1-billion-n75821.

ESPN.com. "Bryce Harper's Retort Goes Viral." June 13, 2012. http://www.espn.com/mlb/story/_/id/8047918/washington-nationals-bryce-harper-clown-question-retort-takes-off.

— — —. "Danica Patrick Voted Most Popular." November 12, 2012. http://www.espn.com/racing/nascar/nationwide/story/_/id/8654189/danica-patrick-voted-nationwide-most-popular-driver.

— — —. "Elijah Holyfield Making a Name for Himself Outside of the Boxing Ring." ESPN video, 3:11. http://www.espn.com/video/clip?id=14696146.

— — —. "NBA History—Rebounds Leaders." http://www.espn.com/nba/history/leaders/_/stat/rebounds.

Feagain, Jon. "Five Ways Color Affects Brand Development." MarketingProfs.com, August 18, 2014. http://www.marketingprofs.com/opinions/2014/25808/five-ways-color-affects-brand-development.

Flanagan, Sarah. "Instafame Has Its Appeal." HuffPost.com, February 21, 2014. http://www.huffingtonpost.com/sarah-flanagan/instafame-vine-instagram-fame_b_4834101.html.

Foudy, Julie, and Drew Thorry. "Danica Patrick: The Art of Racing in a Man's World." ABC News, May 2, 2013. http://abcnews.go.com/Entertainment/danica-patrick-art-racing-mans-world/story?id=19044193.

Fox Sports. "Butch Jones Retweeted Basically Every 2017 Recruit This Morning." August 1, 2016. http://sportsradioknoxville.com/coaches-can-apparently-retweet-recruits-now/.

FoxSports.com. "Staggering 25.4 Million Viewers Witness USA Win Coveted FIFA Women's World Cup 2015 Title." July 6, 2015. http://www.foxsports

.com/presspass/latest-news/2015/07/06/staggering-25-4-million-viewers
-witness-usa-win-coveted-fifa-womens-world-cup-2015-title.

Gaines, Cork. "The Mayweather-Pacquiao Fight Numbers Are In—They
Shattered Expectations by Tens of Millions of Dollars." *Business
Insider*, May 12, 2015. http://www.businessinsider.com/floyd
-mayweather-manny-pacquiao-revenue-2015-5.

— — —. "Marshawn Lynch Reportedly Hasn't Spent a Penny of the $49.7
Million in Salary He Has Made in His NFL Career." *Business Insider*,
February 7, 2016. http://www.businessinsider.com/marshawn-lynch
-saves-nfl-salary-lives-off-endorsements-2016-2.

Garcia, Ahiza. "Pro Athletes and the Things They Trademark." CNNMoney
.com, August 19, 2016. http://money.cnn.com/2016/08/19/news
/trademarks-athletes-usain-bolt-olympics/.

Gerber, Lou. "Battle of the Sexes Was Really a Second Act." *USA Today*,
January 2, 2016. https://www.usatoday.com/story/sports/2016/01/02
/battle-sexes-really-second-act/78086936/.

Gillett, Rachel. "Why We're More Likely to Remember Content with Images
and Video." *Fast Company*, September 18, 2014. https://www
.fastcompany.com/3035856/hit-the-ground-running/why-were-more
-likely-to-remember-content-with-images-and-video-infographics.

GQ. "The 13 Most Stylish Men in the World Right Now." April 18, 2016.
http://www.gq.com/story/most-stylish-men-in-the-world-2016.

Greer, Jordan. "NBA Emoji Chart Gives Perfect Symbols for Past and
Present Stars." *Sporting News*, July 9, 2015. http://www.sportingnews
.com/au/nba/news/emoji-chart-nickname-nba-deandre-jordan
-clippers-paul-pierce-jj-redick/otpqod71vzqw132tvj6nee3cw.

Gustashaw, Megan. "Turns Out Dressing for the Job You Want Actually
Works." *GQ*, February 26, 2016. http://www.gq.com/story/dress-for
-the-job-you-want-office-style.

Hartnett, Tyson. "Why Athletes Go Broke and What We Can Do about It." HuffPost.com, March 5, 2015, updated May 5, 2015. http://www.huffingtonpost.com/tyson-hartnett/why-athletes-go-broke-and_b_6812864.html.

Heid, Markham. "What Your Car Says about You." *Men's Health*, October 20, 2016. https://www.menshealth.com/guy-wisdom/what-your-car-says-about-you.

Hiatt, Brian. "14 Things We Learned about *Straight Outta Compton*." *Rolling Stone*, August 13, 2015. http://www.rollingstone.com/music/news/14-things-we-learned-about-straight-outta-compton-20150813.

Jackson, Bo. Interview by John Brenkus, ESPN Sport Science. YouTube video, 00:26. Posted March 7, 2013. https://www.youtube.com/watch?v=0KASZp_tcWA&app=desktop.

Jenkins, Nash. "David Beckham Chosen as *People* Magazine's Sexiest Man Alive for 2015." *Time*, November 17, 2015. http://time.com/4117758/sexiest-man-alive-2015-people/.

Kadlec, Dan. "What You Have in Common with Bankrupt Pro Athletes." *Time*, June 9, 2016. http://time.com/money/4362102/bankrupt-athletes-lessons-for-you/.

Kaneko, Gemma. "Players, Managers, MLB Alums Pick One Word to Describe Derek Jeter." *Cut4* (blog), September 7, 2014. http://m.mlb.com/cutfour/2014/09/07/93547052/one-word-for-2-derek-jeter.

Keller, Gary, and Jay Papasan. *The One Thing: The Surprisingly Simple Truth behind Extraordinary Results.* Austin, TX: Bard Press, 2013.

Kelly, Brian. "Is the Amex Centurion Card Worth the $2,500 Annual Fee?" ThePointsGuy.com, May 22, 2014. https://thepointsguy.com/2014/05/is-the-amex-centurion-card-worth-the-2500-annual-fee/.

Kerr-Dineen, Luke. "Here Are Your Odds of Becoming a Professional Athlete (They're Not Good)." *For the Win* (blog), *USA Today*, July 27, 2016.

http://ftw.usatoday.com/2016/07/here-are-your-odds-of-becoming
-a-professional-athlete-theyre-not-good.

King, Marquette. "Can I Kick It?" ThePlayersTribune.com, November 7,
2016. https://www.theplayerstribune.com/marquette-king-raiders-can
-i-kick-it/.

Kittaneh, Firas. "Secrets of Succeeding at Visual Marketing on Instagram,
Pinterest and YouTube." *Entrepreneur*, May 18, 2015. https://www
.entrepreneur.com/article/246185.

Kornheiser, Tony. "Off-Broadway Joe: The Song and Dance of a Playboy
Nearing Middle Age." The Stacks, October 24, 2013. http://thestacks
.deadspin.com/off-broadway-joe-the-song-and-dance-of-a-playboy
-neari-1444642189.

Lang, Brett. "Prince Songs and Albums Top iTunes Charts after Singer's
Death." *Variety*, April 21, 2016. http://variety.com/2016/biz/news
/prince-dies-itunes-charts-1201758650/.

Liebman, Glenn. "10 Inspirational Quotes by John Wooden." ESPN.com.
http://www.espn.com/espn/page2/index/_/id/5254520.

Lowry, Brian. "LeBron James Is Truly 'King James' When It Comes to NBA
Finals Ratings." CNNMoney.com, June 1, 2016. http://money.cnn
.com/2016/06/01/media/lebron-james-nba-finals/.

Lozano, Dolores. "Deandre Hopkins Scores First NFL Touchdown in Yeezy
Boost." SB Nation Radio, September 11, 2016. http://www.sbnationradio
.com/deandre-hopkins-scores-first-nfl-touchdown-yeezy-boost/.

Makim, Gareth. "WWE Commentary Legend Jim Ross Describes Conor
McGregor as 'the Perfect Heel.'" SportsJoe.ie, July 2015. https://www
.sportsjoe.ie/mma/wwe-commentary-legend-jim-ross-calls-conor
-mcgregor-the-perfect-heel-29520.

Markovich, Tony. "What the Type of Car You Drive Says about You."
Complex.com, September 9, 2013. http://www.complex.com
/sports/2013/09/what-type-of-car-you-drive-says-about-you/hybrid.

Marshall, Carla. "By 2019, 80% of the World's Internet Traffic Will Be Video [Cisco Study]." TubularInsights.com, June 11, 2015. http://tubularinsights .com/2019-internet-video-traffic/.

Martin, Damon. "Conor McGregor on Floyd Mayweather: 'I Would Most Certainly Dismantle Him.'" FoxSports.com, July 3, 2015. http://www .foxsports.com/ufc/story/ufc-189-conor-mcgregor-on-floyd-mayweather -i-would-most-certainly-dismantle-him-070315.

Martin, Nick. "Why a US Olympian Sold $22K of Ad Space on His Body as a 'Campaign to Be Annoying.'" *Washington Post*, May 7, 2016. https:// www.washingtonpost.com/news/early-lead/wp/2016/05/06/why-an -olympian-sold-22k-of-ad-space-on-his-body-as-a-campaign-to-be -annoying/?utm_term=.6df81db071e7.

Matula, Thaddeus D., dir. "Brian and the Boz." *30 for 30*. Aired October 28, 2014, on ESPN. http://www.espn.com/30for30/film?page =brianandtheboz.

McNary, Dave. "'Straight Outta Compton' Tops $200 Million in Worldwide Box Office." *Variety*, November 2, 2015. http://variety.com/2015/film /news/straight-outta-compton-200-million-box-office-1201631627/.

Miller, Stephen D. "'I Plan to Be a Great Mathematician': An NFL Offensive Lineman Shows He's One of Us." Notices of the AMS 63, no. 2 (February 2016): 148–51. http://dx.doi.org/10.1090/noti1331.

Mink, Ryan. "The Caw: Origin of the Squirrel Dance." Baltimore Ravens' website, January 7, 2013. http://www.baltimoreravens.com/news /article-1/The-Caw-Origin-Of-The-Squirrel-Dance/81d51277-eeb2 -42eb-a6a0-0c7f4b8342e5.

Mitzeliotis, Katrina. "Tommy Hilfiger: Kanye West 'Is a Genius' and 'I Really Respect' Him." HollywoodLife.com, November 3, 2016. http://hollywoodlife.com/2016/11/03/tommy-hilfiger-kanye-west-genius -interview-friend/.

Moyer, Justin Wm. "A Pittsburgh Steeler Wanted to Wear Pink All Season for Breast Cancer. The NFL Said No." *Washington Post*, October 14, 2015. https://www.washingtonpost.com/news/morning-mix/wp/2015/10/14 /a-pittsburgh-steeler-wanted-to-wear-pink-all-season-for-breast -cancer-the-nfl-said-no/?utm_term=.29e71e5ae22d.

Murphy, Mike. "Costliest, Dumbest Tweet of All Time? Laremy Tunsil Probably Lost Millions." Marketwatch.com, April 29, 2016. http://www .marketwatch.com/story/how-many-millions-did-laremy-tunsil-lose -because-of-one-tweet-2016-04-28.

Myers, Gary. "From Deion, 'Boys Receive Prime Praise." *New York Daily News,* January 29, 1996. https://www.nydailynews.com/archives/sports /deion-boys-receive-prime-praise-article-1.713777.

Nathan, Alec. "DeAngelo Williams to Pay for 53 Mammograms to Honor Late Mother." BleacherReport.com, October 13, 2015. http://bleacherreport. com/articles/2578911-deangelo-williams-to-pay-for-53-mammograms -to-honor-late-mother.

Navarra, Matt. "Twitter Is Verifying Way More Accounts, and Here's the Data to Prove It." TheNextWeb.com, July 22, 2016. https://thenextweb.com /twitter/2016/07/22/twitter-verification-rises/#.tnw_LXmKij35.

NBA Encyclopedia Playoff Edition. "Classic NBA Quotes: Magic and Larry." http://www.nba.com/history/Classic_NBA_Quotes_Magic_and_Larry.html.

NCAA. "NCAA Recruiting Facts." July 2016. https://www.ncaa.org/sites /default/files/Recruiting%20Fact%20Sheet%20WEB.pdf.

———. "Estimated Probability of Competing in Professional Athletics." Last updated March 10, 2017. http://www.ncaa.org/about/resources/research /estimated-probability-competing-professional-athletics.

Nelson, Amanda. "15 Seth Godin Quotes to Fuel Spectacular Growth." *Salesforce* (blog), June 15, 2016. https://www.salesforce.com /blog/2016/06/seth-godin-quotes.html.

New Zealand Tourism. "History of the All Black Haka." http://media
.newzealand.com/en/story-ideas/history-of-the-all-black-haka/.

O'Connell, Brian. "How to Get the Amex 'Invite Only' Black Card." The
Street, April 29, 2010. https://www.thestreet.com/story/12805860/1
/how-get-amex-black-card.html.

Ojeda, Louis, Jr. "James Harden: I Wouldn't Shave My Beard for $1 Million."
FoxSports.com, April 16, 2014. http://www.foxsports.com/southwest
/story/james-harden-i-wouldn-t-shave-my-beard-for-1-million-041614.

Paterniti, Michael. "David Beckham on Retirement, Family Life, and
Protecting His Kids." GQ, March 17, 2016. http://www.gq.com/story
/david-beckham-cover-protecting-kids-brooklyn.

Patterson, Chip. "LOOK: LeBron James Gives a King's Share of Signature
Shoes to Ohio State Football." CBSSports.com, August 9, 2016. http://www
.cbssports.com/college-football/news/look-lebron-james-gives-a-kings
-share-of-signature-shoes-to-ohio-state/.

Paulsen. "2016 Ratings Wrap: Despite Down Years, NFL and Olympics
Dominate." SportsMediaWatch.com, January 1, 2017. http://www
.sportsmediawatch.com/2017/01/most-watched-sporting-events
-2016-nfl-olympics-world-series-nba-college-football/3/.

Payne, Dennis. "How Many Contacts Does It Take before Someone
Buys Your Product?" Business Insider, July 12, 2011. http://www
.businessinsider.com/how-many-contacts-does-it-take-before
-someone-buys-your-product-2011-7.

Payne, Marissa. "Ohio State's Ezekiel Elliott Wants to Trademark 'Hero in a
Half-Shirt.'" Washington Post, August 29, 2015. https://www.washingtonpost
.com/news/early-lead/wp/2015/08/29/ohio-states-ezekiel-elliott-wants
-to-trademark-hero-in-a-half-shirt/?utm_term=.a64a2e3ac352.

Perlberg, Steven. "NCAA Championship Audience Falls to 17.8 Million in
Cable Debut." Wall Street Journal, April 5, 2016. https://www.wsj.com

/articles/ncaa-championship-audience-falls-to-17-8-million-in-cable
-debut-1459883628.

Phillips, Gary. "Reflecting on All That Derek Jeter Was." BleacherReport
.com, September 28, 2014. http://bleacherreport.com/articles/2190547.

Players' Tribune, The. "About." Accessed November 8, 2017. https://www
.theplayerstribune.com/about/.

Popsugar. "Billie Jean King Has Always Been a Champ for Women's Rights."
YouTube video, May 19, 2017. https://www.youtube.com/watch?v
=QbmFWC3moDM.

Robinson, Jackie. Interview by Dick Cavett, *The Dick Cavett Show*. YouTube
video, 14:58. Posted April 28, 2017. https://www.youtube.com/watch?v
=YCr0RAzf8ds.

Robinson, Will. "Rocky IV Turns 30: Here Are 4 Things You Never Knew
about the Film." *Entertainment Weekly*, November 27, 2015. http://ew
.com/article/2015/11/27/rocky-iv-30th-anniversary-things-you
-didnt-know/.

Rossen, Jake. "Adjusted for Inflation: A History of the Reebok Pump."
Mental Floss, October 22, 2015. http://mentalfloss.com/article/69922
/adjusted-inflation-history-reebok-pump.

RottenTomotoes.com. Review of *Rocky IV*. Directed by Sylvester Stallone.
https://www.rottentomatoes.com/m/rocky_iv.

Rubenstein, Alan. "The Top Twenty Individual Rivalries in Sports."
BleacherReport.com, July 7, 2010. http://bleacherreport.com
/articles/416871-the-top-twenty-rivalries-in-sports.

Rush, Brianne Carlon. "Science of Storytelling: Why and How to Use It in
Your Marketing." *Guardian*, August 28, 2014. https://www
.theguardian.com/media-network/media-network-blog/2014/aug
/28/science-storytelling-digital-marketing.

Samano, Simon. "Ray Lewis Shares the Origins of His 'Squirrel' Dance." *USA Today*, January 6, 2013. https://www.usatoday.com/story /gameon/2013/01/06/ravens-ray-lewis-squirrel-dance/1812555/.

Sandomir, Richard. "Tyson's Bankruptcy Is a Lesson in Ways to Squander a Fortune." *New York Times*, August 5, 2003. http://www.nytimes.com/2003 /08/05/sports/tyson-s-bankruptcy-is-a-lesson-in-ways-to-squander-a -fortune.html.

Scaggs, Austin. "Kanye West: A Genius in Praise of Himself." *Rolling Stone*, September 20, 2007. http://www.rollingstone.com/music/news /kanye-west-a-genius-in-praise-of-himself-20070920.

Schoenwald, Christine. "What Your Favorite Go-To Clothing Color Says About You Personality [*sic*]." HuffPost.com, October 16, 2015. http:// www.huffingtonpost.com/yourtango/go-to-clothing-color_b_8286140 .html.

Schwartz, Larry. "Namath Was Lovable Rogue." ESPN Classic. http://www .espn.com/classic/biography/s/namath_joe.html.

Schwartz, Nick. "The Average Career Earnings of Athletes across America's Major Sports Will Shock You." *For the Win* (blog), *USA Today*, October 24, 2013. http://ftw.usatoday.com/2013/10/average-career-earnings-nfl-nba -mlb-nhl-mls.

Scott, Nate. "Kanye West Is a Jerk (Who Is Also a Genius)." *USA Today*, February 12, 2016. http://ftw.usatoday.com/2016/02/kanye-west-is-a -jerk-who-is-also-a-genius-the-life-of-pablo-yeezy-season-3.

Shaul, Brandy. "Report: 92% of Online Consumers Use Emoji (Infographic)." *Adweek*, September 30, 2015. http://www.adweek.com/digital /report-92-of-online-consumers-use-emoji-infographic/.

Sloan, Jordan Taylor. "Johnny Cash Did More for Today's Music than You Probably Even Realize." Mic, December 9, 2014. https://mic.com /articles/105954/johnny-cash-did-more-for-today-s-music-than-you -probably-even-realize#.Nem1986dX.

Spikes. "Floppin' Heck!" November 28, 2014. https://spikes.iaaf.org/post
/dick-fosbury-tells-spikes-why-its-called-the.

SportingNews.com "See King James' Newest Shoe: The Nike LeBron 13."
http://www.sportingnews.com/nba/photos/lebron-13-shoes-photos
-colorways-release-dates/ofz7l2iaonj91r90vcik4viy6.

Statista. "Highest-Rated Televised NCAA Basketball National
Championship Games from 1975–2016." 2017. https://www.statista.com
/statistics/219645/ncaa-basketball-tournament-games-by-tv-ratings/.

Steinberg, Leigh. "5 Reasons Why 80% of Retired NFL Players Go Broke."
Forbes, February 9, 2015. https://www.forbes.com/sites/leighsteinberg
/2015/02/09/5-reasons-why-80-of-retired-nfl-players-go-broke
/#70151a7778cc.

Stern, Steven, writer. Babe Ruth. Produced by Ross Greenburg, Rick
Bernstein, George Roy, and Steven Stern. Aired August 16, 1998.

Takeda, Allison. "Kanye West Compares North to 'the Prince and Princess
in London,' Wanted Bound 2 to Look 'Phony.'" US Weekly, November 27,
2013. http://www.usmagazine.com/entertainment/news/kanye-west
-compares-north-to-the-prince-and-princess-in-london-wanted-bound
-2-to-look-phony-20132711.

Torre, Pablo S. "How (and Why) Athletes Go Broke." Sports Illustrated,
March 23, 2009. https://www.si.com/vault/2009/03/23/105789480
/how-and-why-athletes-go-broke?xid=huffpo.

Twitter. "About Verified Accounts." 2017. https://support.twitter.com
/articles/119135#.

USA Today. "30 of Muhammad Ali's Best Quotes." June 3, 2016, updated
June 5, 2016. https://www.usatoday.com/story/sports/boxing/2016
/06/03/muhammad-ali-best-quotes-boxing/85370850/.

Ward, Austin. "Ezekiel Elliott Scoffs at Jersey Rule." ESPN.com, April 2,
2015. http://www.espn.com/college-football/story/_/id/12605826
/ezekiel-elliott-ohio-state-buckeyes-says-crop-top-jersey-rule-silly.

Warner, Ralph, et al. "The 50 Cockiest Athletes of All Time." Complex.com, June 1, 2012. http://www.complex.com/sports/2012/06/the-50-cockiest -athletes-of-all-time/.

Webster, Danny. "Floyd Mayweather Says He Started Conor McGregor Fight Rumors." BleacherReport.com, May 8, 2016. http://bleacherreport.com /articles/2638839-floyd-mayweather-says-he-started-conor-mcgregor -fight-rumors.

Weingarten, Gene. "Pearls Before Breakfast: Can One of the Nation's Great Musicians Cut through the Fog of a DC Rush Hour? Let's Find Out." *Washington Post*, April 8, 2007. https://www.washingtonpost.com /lifestyle/magazine/pearls-before-breakfast-can-one-of-the-nations -great-musicians-cut-through-the-fog-of-a-dc-rush-hour-lets-find -out/2014/09/23/8a6d46da-4331-11e4-b47c-f5889e061e5f_story .html?utm_term=.1585a25be4ee.

Weisman, Aly. "Elon Musk Explains the Genius of Kanye West." *Inc.*, April 17, 2015. https://www.inc.com/business-insider/elon-musk-explains -the-genius-of-kanye-west.html.

West, Kanye. "Diamonds from Sierra Leone (Remix)." Featuring Jay-Z. Track 13 on *Late Registration*. Roc-A-Fella Records, 2005.

Williams, Alex. "Odell Beckham Jr. Responds to the Lena Dunham Dust-Up: 'I Have to Learn More about the Situation.'" *New York Times*, September 7, 2016. https://www.nytimes.com/2016/09/08/fashion/odell-beckham-jr -lena-dunham-met-gala-response.html.

Williams, Doug. "Athletes Trademarking the Phrase That Pays." ESPN .com, July 24, 2012. http://www.espn.com/blog/playbook/fandom/post /_/id/6108#more.

Wilson, Ryan. "Rob Gronkowski: I Haven't Spent One Dime of My NFL Earnings." CBSSports.com, June 22, 2015. http://www.cbssports.com /nfl/news/rob-gronkowski-i-havent-spent-one-dime-of-my-nfl-earnings/.

Wong, Alex. "Best Slam Dunk Contest Moments Ever." SportsOnEarth.com, February 17, 2017. http://www.sportsonearth.com/article/216256214 /best-slam-dunks-in-history_3.

Woodward, Ellie, and Rebecca Hendin. "How the Kardashians Manipulated the Media to Become the Most Famous Family in the World." BuzzFeed .com, September 25, 2015. https://www.buzzfeed.com/elliewoodward /how-the-kardashians-manipulated-the-media-to-become-the-most.

World Rugby. "The Greatest Haka EVER?" YouTube video. https://www .youtube.com/watch?v=yiKFYTFJ_kw.

Yuscavage, Chris. "Watch Damian Lillard Drop Bars in Front of an Excited Gary Busey on 'Sway in the Morning.'" Complex.com, November 22, 2016. http://www.complex.com/sports/2016/11/damian-lillard-drop-bars -gary-busey-sway-in-the-morning.

about the author

Jeremy Darlow is a leading brand consultant, former director of marketing for adidas football and baseball, adjunct marketing professor, and author of the book *Brands Win Championships*, a branding guidebook for college sports programs. During and since his role at adidas, he has worked with some of the most heralded athletes, celebrities, and NCAA programs in and around sports, including Aaron Rodgers, Von Miller, Adrian Peterson, Dak Prescott, Kris Bryant, Carlos Correa, Lionel Messi, Dale Earnhardt, Jr., Snoop Dogg, Kanye West, Notre Dame, Michigan, UCLA, Miami, Nebraska, Wisconsin, and Texas A&M. His first book has been read and studied by the heads of major college sports programs across the United States, including Georgetown University, Gonzaga University, the University of Alabama, the University of Louisville, Oregon State University, and New York University. He lives in Portland, Oregon.